OCS Study MMS 2005-025

Annual Assessment of Subsistence Bowhead Whaling Near Cross Island, 2003: ANIMIDA Task 4 Annual Report

Contract Number 1435-01-99-CT-30998, TO 10904

Prepared for:
U.S. Department of the Interior
Minerals Management Service
Alaska Outer Continental Shelf Region
Anchorage, AK

Prepared by:
Michael Galginaitis
Applied Sociocultural Research
Anchorage, AK

Dale Funk
LGL Alaska Research Associates Inc.
Anchorage, AK

May 2005

U.S. Department of the Interior
Minerals Management Service
Alaska Outer Continental Shelf Region

The Department of the Interior Mission

As the Nation's principal conservation agency, the Department of the Interior has responsibility for most of our nationally owned public lands and natural resources. This includes fostering sound use of our land and water resources; protecting our fish, wildlife, and biological diversity; preserving the environmental and cultural values of our national parks and historical places; and providing for the enjoyment of life through outdoor recreation. The Department assesses our energy and mineral resources and works to ensure that their development is in the best interests of all our people by encouraging stewardship and citizen participation in their care. The Department also has a major responsibility for American Indian reservation communities and for people who live in island territories under U.S. administration.

The Minerals Management Service Mission

As a bureau of the Department of the Interior, the Minerals Management Service's (MMS) primary responsibilities are to manage the mineral resources located on the Nation's Outer Continental Shelf (OCS), collect revenue from the Federal OCS and onshore Federal and Indian lands, and distribute those revenues.

Moreover, in working to meet its responsibilities, the **Offshore Minerals Management Program** administers the OCS competitive leasing program and oversees the safe and environmentally sound exploration and production of our Nation's offshore natural gas, oil and other mineral resources. The MMS **Royalty Management Program** meets its responsibilities by ensuring the efficient, timely and accurate collection and disbursement of revenue from mineral leasing and production due to Indian tribes and allottees, States and the U.S. Treasury.

The MMS strives to fulfill its responsibilities through the general guiding principles of: (1) being responsive to the public's concerns and interests by maintaining a dialogue with all potentially affected parties and (2) carrying out its programs with an emphasis on working to enhance the quality of life for all Americans by lending MMS assistance and expertise to economic development and environmental protection.

Annual Assessment of Subsistence Bowhead Whaling Near Cross Island, 2003: ANIMIDA Task 4 Annual Report

Contract Number 1435-01-99-CT-30998, TO 10904

Prepared for:
U.S. Department of the Interior
Minerals Management Service
Alaska Outer Continental Shelf Region
Anchorage, AK

Prepared by:
Michael Galginaitis[1], Dale W. Funk[2]

[1]Applied Sociocultural Research
608 West Fourth Avenue, Suite 31
Post Office Box 99510-1352
Anchorage, AK 99510-1352

[2]LGL Alaska Research Associates Inc.
1101 East 76th Avenue, Suite B
Anchorage, AK 99518

May 2005

This study was funded by the U.S. Department of the Interior, Minerals Management Service (MMS), Alaska Outer Continental Shelf Region, Anchorage, Alaska under Contract No. 1435-01-99-CT-30998, TO 10904, as part of the MMS Alaska Environmental Studies Program

Executive Summary

This Task Order, funded by the Minerals Management Service (MMS) has as its broad objective the description of subsistence whaling as currently conducted near Cross Island by residents of Nuiqsut. This effort is designed to measure basic descriptive parameters of Cross Island whaling so that observed changes (if any) can be analyzed in relation to such factors as oil and gas activities, weather and ice conditions, or other variables. Special attention is devoted to geospatial information through the sharing of GIS information by participating whaling crews. Project reports are only for the purposes of reporting information collected, with no analysis of the information either as a self-contained database or in conjunction with the many pertinent external databases. As a second broad objective, the project is designed as a collaborative effort of MMS and its contractor, Applied Sociocultural Research (ASR), the subsistence whalers from Nuiqsut, and the Alaska Eskimo Whaling Commission (AEWC). The project will develop a system for collecting information that local whalers themselves can adopt, adapt, and maintain. This report documents the results of the third and final year of this component of the ANIMIDA project. It will be continued by at least three (possibly four) years of additional data collection as a component of the cANIMIDA project.

Three methods of information collection are employed – systematic observations, collection of daily vessel locational information from handheld GPS units, and whalers' self-reports and perceptions. Emphasis has been placed on such measures as:
- Number of crews actively whaling (observation)
- Size and composition of crews, and fluctuation over the whaling season (observation)
- Number of whales harvested (observation, self-report)
- Days spent whaling, and days prevented from whaling (weather, equipment failure or repair, etc.) (observation, self-report)
- Days suitable for whaling when whaling did not occur (observation, self-report)
- Subsistence activities occurring other than whaling (self-report, observation)
- Location of whale sightings and whale harvest (GPS, self-report)
- Location of whale searching (GPS, self-report)
- Local weather and ice conditions (observation, self-report)
- Bowhead whale behavior in the Cross Island area, and indicated differences from past experience (self-report)
- Changes in access or other issues related to the whale hunt, such as increased effort for the same (or reduced) harvest, increased risk, increased cost (self-report)

In 2003, four crews from Nuiqsut whaled from Cross Island. At least two boats went whaling on seven different days. At least one crew was on Cross Island a total of nineteen days (counting day of arrival and day of departure). Weather prevented whaling on seven days, three days were devoted to butchering and preparations to leave Cross Island after the community quota was taken, and two days were devoted to travel. Four whales were harvested. Weather conditions were poor during the 2003 season, and Nuiqsut whalers scouted for whales on all days when conditions allowed (including the day after the first whale was taken). The final three whales were taken in two days and butchered in sequence. The number of crew members in each vessel scouting for whales varied 2 to 6 per boat per day (most commonly 3 or 4). Scouting trips varied in duration from one hour nine minutes to nine hours six minutes. Total trip distance varied from 25 to 66 miles (with the exception of aborted trips due to mechanical problems) with a greatest distance from Cross Island of from 5.5 to 22.6 miles. Whales were struck from 5.2 to 12.2 (average 9.3) miles from Cross Island. Other daily trip characteristics -- GPS tracks, marked points, self-report of significant sightings, and other perceptions – were also collected and are discussed in the report.

Table of Contents

List of Tables and Figures

Acronyms and Abbreviations Used in Tables, Text, and Appendices

Acronym or Abbreviation	Expanded Term or Reference
AA[1]	Akiviana Whaling Crew
BO[1]	Oyagak Whaling Crew
IAN	Aqargiun Whaling Crew
NAP[1]	Napageak Whaling Crew
NUK[1]	Nukapigak Whaling Crew
#	Number
ACS	Alaska Clean Seas
AEWC	Alaska Eskimo Whaling Commission
ANCSA	Alaska Native Claims Settlement Act
ANIMIDA	Arctic Nearshore Impact Monitoring in Development Area
BP	Barometric Pressure
BPXA	British Petroleum Exploration Alaska
cANIMIDA	continuation of ANIMIDA
CI	Cross Island
esp.	especially
F	Fahrenheit (temperature measurement)
FDFCI	Farthest Distance From Cross Island (during a boat trip)
ft	Feet
GIS	Geographical Information System
GPS	Geographic Positioning System
HCC	High Cloud Cover
HP	Horse Power
IHLC	Inupiat History, Language, and Culture Commission
IWC	International Whaling Commission
MFCI	Miles From Cross Island
mmddyy	Date Format – month/day/year
MMS	Minerals management Service
MPH	Miles Per Hour
N,S,E,W and combinations	Compass directions (north, south, east, west, northeast, etc)
NA	Not Applicable
NQT	Nuiqsut
NSB	North Slope Borough
NSB DW	North Slope Borough Department of Wildlife Management
OCS	Outer Continental Shelf
OWA	Oil/Whalers Agreement
TOT	Total Time (of individual boat trips)
UNK	Unknown
w/number or /number	With the specified number (of people)
WCA	Whaling Captains Association
WCC	Whaling Communication Center
WD	West Dock (Prudhoe Bay)
WF	Weather File (time series of weather station measurements)

[1]When crews use multiple boats, each boat is differentiated by a number after the crew designation (1-4)

Preface

While this project is conceptually simple and straightforward, the logistics and funding history have been more complicated. It was implemented as a 3-year field effort as a component of the ANIMIDA program, with annual reports and a summary final report. Because of delays in the final approval of the program and the time necessary to properly consult with Nuiqsut and other North Slope research participants, only two field seasons (2001-2002) were possible within the timeframe of the original ANIMIDA program. It was anticipated that the ANIMIDA program would be continued as cANIMIDA, but that the procurement process would not be accomplished until after the 2003 field season. Thus, an additional field season (2003) was added as a contract modification to the ANIMIDA contract. The cANIMIDA program, once approved, funded field work for 2004-2006, with an option for an additional year of data collection for 2007, with an analytical synthetic report treating the full time series of data. Thus, this is the third annual report on the Cross Island fieldwork, and the final year of ANIMIDA, of what will be a time series of at least six such reports, to be followed by a single overall analytical report.

The 2003 Annual Report consists of several parts:
- The main body of the report, provided in hard copy and in electronic form (PDF) on the CD-ROM accompanying the report;
- Appendix A, Daily Boat Report Forms for 2003 – in electronic form (PDF) only, on the CD-ROM accompanying the report;
- Appendix B, Daily Boat GPS Tracks for 2003, displayed as figures – in electronic form (PDF) only, on the CD-ROM accompanying the report; and
- Cross Island Weather File for 2003 – in electronic form (Excel) only, on the CD-ROM accompanying the report.
- The processed GPS files, in original MapSource form and as DXF files, are held by the MMS Alaska OCS Region and are not distributed as part of the annual report.

Products previously produced for this project have been:
- 2001 ANIMIDA Task Order 4 Annual Report (Galginaitis and Funk 2004a)
- 2002 ANIMIDA Task Order 4 Annual Report (Galginaitis and Funk 2004b)
- ANIMIDA Task Order 4 Final Report (Galginaitis and Funk 2005)
- Presentation at the Alaska Outer Continental Shelf Region 9th Information Transfer Meeting (3/12/03 in Anchorage, 3/14/03 in Barrow)
- Presentation at the SETAC 24th Annual Meeting (11/12/03 in Austin, Texas)
- Presentation at the Alaska Outer Continental Shelf Region 10th Information Transfer Meeting (3/16/03 in Anchorage, 3/18/03 in Barrow).

The 2004 Annual Report is in preparation.

Acknowledgments

This work would not have been possible without the assistance of a great number of people. Foremost among them must be the whalers and other residents of Nuiqsut. While it is unfair to single out individuals when all provided essential information and support in what is after all a communal and cooperative undertaking, I would be remiss if I did not explicitly thank those whaling captains and their crews who extended me the hospitality of their cabins. This is the report on my third field season on Cross Island, for which Billy Oyagak served as a most gracious host. Paul Kittick, as my host for the first year when the project was still an unknown quantity to the whalers, also has my utmost appreciation. Archie Ahkiviana has my gratitude for hosting me the second year. I of course also thank the other crews who were out on Cross Island for the 2001-2003 seasons (Napageak, Nukapigak, and Aqargiun), and David Pausanna for all the help he gave me over the phone and while I was in Nuiqsut. I cannot begin to list the other residents of Nuiqsut who shared much more of their time and knowledge than I had any reason to expect. Maggie Ahmaogak of the AEWC also gave her advice, support, and cooperation.

Industry also provided a good deal of help in various forms, from advice to more concrete logistical support. Ray Jucubczak, and Concie Rock at BPXA were especially notable in this regard, although several individuals at Alaska Clean Seas were also very helpful. BPXA also assisting with the transformation of the raw GPS track information into more usable GPS-based maps for the 2001-2003 data.

MMS, as the sponsor of the project, also deserves a formal "Thank you." Dick Prentki has been an ideal COTR, even though the course of the project has not always been smooth.

Lastly, the entities for which ASR performed this work as a subcontractor, LGL Limited of Alaska and Batelle, must be thanked for their willingness to trust that the work would be accomplished with a minimum of oversight on their part. The budget for this limited task would not support a good deal of administrative overhead, and both worked with me to make it work. I am especially grateful to Dale Funk at LGL.

The above notwithstanding, all errors and shortcomings of this report are the responsibility of Michael Galginaitis and ASR. Please advise me of as many as you find, so that whatever effort continues in this regard can bear as much fruit as possible. In this regard, three additional years of data collection have been funded, 2004-2006. Information for 2004 is being processed, and plans are being made for the 2005 work as this 2003 report is finalized. But again, none of this work would be possible without the cooperation and support of the Nuiqsut whalers, to whom I again give my most profound thanks.

Introduction and Objectives of the Task Order

This Task Order, funded by the Minerals management Service (MMS) has as its broad objective the description of subsistence whaling as currently conducted near Cross Island by residents of Nuiqsut. It is the only socioeconomic component of the ANIMIDA program, which focuses more on physical science. While "traditional" subsistence whaling has been well documented in a number of locations, contemporary subsistence whaling is not as well documented, especially in terms of changes over time. This effort is designed to measure basic parameters of Cross Island whaling so that observed changes (if any) can in the future be analyzed in relation to such factors as oil and gas activities, weather and ice conditions, or other variables. Observations, and the narrative annual report summarizing them, will focus on descriptive measures of activities associated with whaling. Special attention is devoted to geospatial information through the sharing of GIS information by participating whaling crews. Project reports are only for the purposes of reporting information collected, with no analysis of the information either as a self-contained database or in conjunction with external databases. Among the many external databases of potential pertinence to the descriptive information collected under this task order are the Human Activities Database (another MMS project) and remote sensing information on ice cover or other geophysical parameters. Other linkages for potential future analysis (AEWC records of whale harvest, or untranscribed IHLC tapes, for example) also exist.

As a second broad objective, the project is designed as a collaborative effort among MMS (and its contractor, Applied Sociocultural Research), the subsistence whalers from Nuiqsut, and the Alaska Eskimo Whaling Commission (AEWC). Beyond the goal of three years of descriptive information on Cross Island subsistence whaling activities, the project was to develop a system for collecting such information that local whalers themselves could adopt, adapt, and maintain. The methodology has now been developed sufficiently, but the transition to local implementation of the program will occur in the next three years.

This is the third and final field season for this task as part of the ANIMIDA project, but it will continue for an additional three years as a component of the cANIMIDA program (which continues most parts of the ANIMIDA program). Annual reports will be produced for the 2004, 2005, and 2006 field seasons. A more analytical report summarizing and analyzing the full six years of data (2001-2006) will also be produced.

An Overview of Contemporary Subsistence Whaling in Alaska

The Inupiat of the North Slope maintain and enjoy a vital culture -- with kinship, dependence on hunting wildlife resources, and a respectful relationship to the land as fundamental values. Hunting provides most of the meat consumed by Inupiat. Whaling not only provides a significant part of this food, but is also a key social organizational activity for North Slope Inupiat. Whaling is also a central ideological idiom for the expression of key cultural values, and an important vehicle for the transmission of those values (Worl 1980, Rexford 1997). Subsistence whaling has been (and continues to be) a key focus for Inupiat and Yupik culture and society (Bering Straits area, Northern coastal Alaska) for at least 1,000 to 1,500 years (Dumond 1984, Krupnik and Stoker 1993, McCartney 1994). However, nothing more than a brief orientation to contemporary subsistence whaling in Alaska is attempted in this report, and references are illustrative, not exhaustive. This discussion provides only a general description of some key aspects of the organization of subsistence whaling, within the context of its management regime, that are important for an understanding of this project's methods and results. This discussion proceeds from the general to the more specific.

In Alaska, ten coastal communities currently field whaling crews and are members of the Alaska Eskimo Whaling Commission (AEWC). The AEWC was formed in 1977 in direct response to the International Whaling Commission's (IWC) decision to ban the Alaskan subsistence bowhead whale hunt. The IWC had two main concerns – that the bowhead whale population was too small to sustain a regular harvest, and that subsistence hunting methods were too wasteful (too many animals were killed but then "lost"). As a result of a complicated series of negotiations, the United States and the AEWC convinced the IWC to allocate an initially small quota of bowheads that could be harvested in 1978. This quota was accompanied by an data collection program to measure and monitor the bowhead whale population and the efficiency of subsistence whaling harvest. This has resulted in an increased confidence in the robust size of the bowhead whale population and an ever-increasing quota of animals available for harvest. It has also created an incentive for the reduction of "struck and lost" whales which has been quite successful. Currently AEWC co-manages the Alaskan subsistence bowhead whale hunt with the United States Government, and this management regime is consistently cited as one of the most successful examples of such management. Huntington 1992 provides a useful analytical discussion of these developments. The original decision documents for the 1978 IWC action (U.S. Department of Commerce 1978, FEIS) also contain much of interest.

The IWC sets an overall quota for the hunt, and the AEWC in turn allocates that quota among the whaling communities. Each whaling community is represented by a local Whaling Captains Association (WCA) at the AEWC, and each local WCA is responsible for managing the hunt in its respective community. Nuiqsut initially received an allocation of one whale or one strike (whichever occurred first) for 1978. Its current allocation is three whales or three strikes. Unused strikes and quota can be transferred between communities, quota is now allocated in multi-year blocks, and there can be some "roll-over" of quota from one year to the next. Thus, the harvest in some years for any given community may be greater than the "normal" quota allocated.

Subsistence whaling in Alaska occurs in the spring (generally April-May) and the fall (generally September-October), when the bowhead whale migration brings them reasonably close to the whaling communities. In the spring, bowhead whales migrate north through the Bering Strait and then, in Alaskan waters, east of Point Barrow into Canadian waters, where they spend the summer (some also go west into Russian waters). In the fall they reverse this course. Spring whaling differs from fall whaling. In the spring whales are migrating through relatively narrow open leads in the ice whereas in the fall the water is generally more open (although there is often thick floating ice). Spring leads do not open up close enough to Nuiqsut or Kaktovik to allow these communities to whale in the spring. In the fall, because whales are not confined by leads, it is difficult in most years for whaling communities south of Barrow to whale (although St. Lawrence Island and Wainwright whalers have taken a few whales in the fall), since the whales are so far offshore at those points. Thus most whaling communities whale in the spring. Barrow whales in both the spring and the fall. Nuiqsut and Kaktovik whale only in the fall. Spring whalers have traditionally and historically used only skin boats (until recently), whereas fall whalers use more durable wood, aluminum, and fiberglass boats. This is related to three general seasonal differences: the greater need to avoid unnecessary noise in the spring, the harsher environmental conditions of fall whaling (rougher seas, more floating ice), and the greater need for speed in the fall to find and pursue whales in more open water. Recent changes in spring whaling, especially in Barrow, have been described and discussed in Wohlforth (2004), and interested readers are referred to that source. This report concentrates on fall whaling by Nuiqsut residents, currently conducted from and near Cross Island.

The Historical Context of Cross Island Whaling

The present community of Nuiqsut has a relatively short history, having been resettled in 1973. However, Inupiat use and occupation of the Nuiqsut area has a very long history, which is the basis for Nuiqsut's status as a village recognized under the Alaska Native Claims Settlement Act (ANCSA). Nuiqsut is located about 12 miles inland on the Colville River (Figure 1), which is not a typical location for a whaling community. However, its residents trace their ancestry to people who whaled in the mid-Beaufort Sea (including near Cross Island) in the first half of the twentieth century, as well as prior to that time. Treatments of the complex and dynamic history of the North Slope region in general, and the Nuiqsut area in particular, can be found in Brown 1979, Galginaitis et al. 1984, Hoffman et al. 1987, Galginaitis 1990, and Long 1996. These sources are the basis for the information in this section. Figure 1 shows the location of Nuiqsut on the Colville River, and Cross Island in the Beaufort Sea, as well as typical routes between Nuiqsut and Cross Island and some significant landmarks in between. Cross Island is about 73 miles northeast of Nuiqsut "as the crow flies" and from 92 to 109 miles away by boat, depending on which channel of the Colville River can be used to reach the ocean. When the water level in the river is high, the more direct route can be used. When the water level is low, the more direct river channel is too shallow for most boats, so the longer route is used. Cross Island itself is about eleven miles offshore, but more importantly from a logistical point of view is ten miles from the Endicott causeway and fifteen miles from West Dock.

Prehistoric use of Cross Island has not been well documented or investigated archaeologically, but documentation for more recent use is quite extensive. Families who lived on and used Cross Island seasonally during the first half of the twentieth century included the Woods, Pausanna, Saavgaq, Ulaaq, Ahsoak, Ahgook, Ikpikuk, Ahvakana, Akpik, Sovalik, Kaigelak, Tigulak, Ahsogeak, Ahkivgak, Ekolook, and Ekowana (Smith 1980). Perhaps most important in terms of whaling was Taaqpak, who used Cross Island as a whaling base from the early twentieth century through the late 1940s. Documentation for his whaling harvests is quite incomplete, but include accounts of whales taken near Cross Island in 1922, 1927, 1928, and 1938. Many of today's active whalers learned from Taaqpak or those who were on his crews. In turn, Taaqpak maintained that Inupiat had hunted whales near Cross Island for centuries (Carnahan 1979:21-31). Thus whaling near Cross Island has a strong cultural continuity.

When Nuiqsut was resettled in 1973, many of the original settlers traveled from Barrow with the supplies necessary for their life in tents for a year or more. They used a variety of means – sleds towed by a small Cat (a tractor with tracks), snow machines, and weasels (another sort of tracked

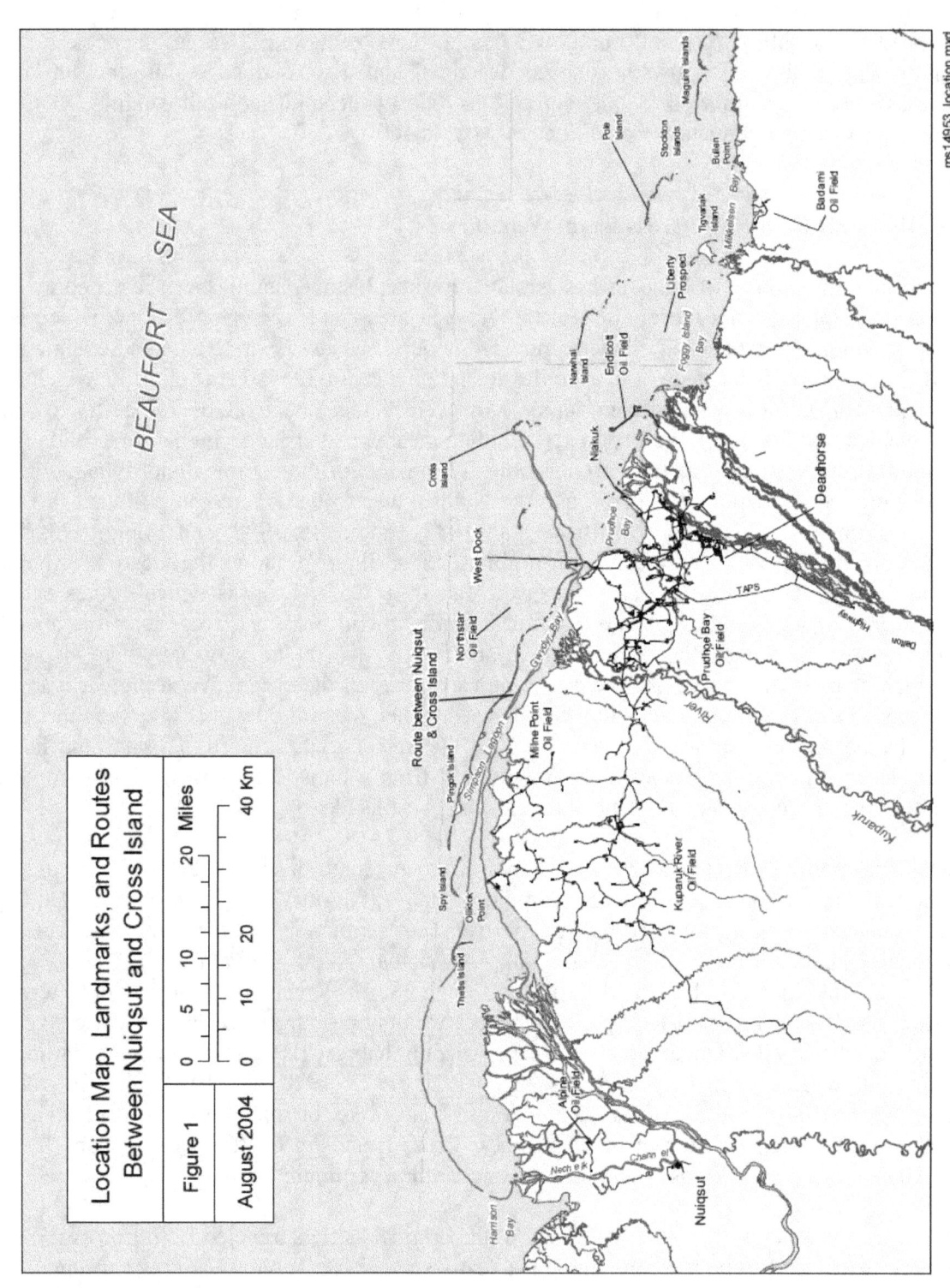

Location Map, Landmarks, and Routes Between Nuiqsut and Cross Island

Figure 1				
	0	5	10	20 Miles
August 2004	0	10	20	40 Km

BEAUFORT SEA

ms14953_location.mxd

vehicle, of WW II vintage). One of these original founders took the first whale for Nuiqsut that fall, while on his way to Kaktovik to obtain some muktuk and meat to take back to the village. He and his crew had been looking for whales and had been out about six weeks. They had not seen any whales in that time, although they had seen a great number of seals, which was about their only source of food after the third week of their trip. By the sixth week the whaling captain had concluded that they were too late – that the whales had either passed them by or were too far from the shore. On the chance that Kaktovik whalers had been more successful, he decided to go to Kaktovik to obtain some muktuk and meat to take back to Nuiqsut. They then came upon a whale in the Brownlow Point/Flaxman Island area, in shallow water. They took this whale, butchered it, and returned to Nuiqsut with as much as possible. Several boats from Nuiqsut then made another trip to the harvest site to recover more of the muktuk.

Most of the six members of this 1973 crew are now active Nuiqsut whalers, and the captain remains one of the most active Nuiqsut whalers. In the years after 1973 relatively few crews whaled from Nuiqsut, with relatively infrequent success. Nuiqsut whalers regularly went to other communities in the spring to participate in spring whaling (a pattern that some continue up through the present – Pausanna, personal communication). The next Nuiqsut whale was not taken until 1982, although crews whaled from various locations between 1973 and 1982 – Pingok Island, Narwhal Island, and Cross Island among them. A summary of whale harvest by Nuiqsut crews is presented in Table 1 below. Nuiqsut whalers attribute at least part of their relative lack of success in the 1970s and 1980s to interference from oil and gas exploration, as well as poor weather and ice conditions in some years, and a difficult logistical situation. These factors are also evident in the three years with the greatest incidence of "struck and lost" whales (1989- 1991 or 1992). Once Cross Island was established as a logistical center for Nuiqsut whaling, and Nuiqsut whalers gained experience there, harvest success became much more regular – although another factor is more moderate ice conditions.

Cross Island is a low sandy barrier island with an artificial higher area built from gravel. This higher area was constructed for past oil and gas exploratory drilling. Cross Island is about 3 miles long and 150 yards wide, and is constantly changing due to erosion and redeposition. Especially in the earlier years logistical support for whaling on Cross Island was very difficult. Whalers had to haul or find their own gas and water, and hunted and fished to provide most or all of their food. There was at most one cabin for however many people were whaling. Since the mid-1980s, with the advent of the Oil-Whalers Agreement (OWA) in 1986 between the oil industry and fall whalers (represented by the AEWC), logistical considerations have become somewhat easier. The oil and gas industry (and especially BPXA) has been providing logistical support of various sorts to Nuiqsut whalers as a mitigation measure for potentially disrupting subsistence whaling by exploration, development, and/or production activities.

At the most basic level, the OWA provides for the constant communication between industry and the whalers about all of their respective ongoing activities, so that each can avoid interfering with the other. The mechanism for this mutual communication is the Whaling Communication Center (WCC – also referred to as the Conflict Avoidance Communication Center or the Oil/Whalers Communications Center) in Deadhorse. The WCC operates during

Table 1: Recent Harvest of Bowhead Whales Near Cross Island

Year	Whales			Notes
	Quota	Landed	Struck & Lost	
1973	NA	1	0	
1982	1	1	0	
1986		1	0	
1987		1	0	
1989		2	2	Oil industry vessel disturbance noted
1990		0	1	Oil industry disturbance, also rough seas
1991	3	1	2	Poor weather, bad ice conditions
1992	3	2	1	
1993	3	3	0	Very favorable conditions
1995	4	4	0	
1996	4	2	0	
1997	4	3	1	
1998	4	4	1	
1999	4	3	0	
2000	4	4	0	Very favorable conditions
2001	4	3	0	
2002	4	4	1	
2003	4	4	0	
Notes: Years of no harvest and no "struck and lost" are not listed. This does not imply that no whaling effort was made that year. "Quota" was not applicable in 1973. Source: Compiled from AWC records, personal communications from Nuiqsut whalers, and field notes from the 2001-2003 whaling seasons				

each fall whaling season and is staffed by bilingual radio operators, with at least one from Nuiqsut and one from Kaktovik. All industry and whaling vessels are required to report their activities to the WCC in real time (purpose, time left, time returned, significant events as they occur), and the WCC maintains a log of these reports which is archived by the AEWC. This provides a record of activities as they take place, and also documents to some extent the whaling activities. It also allows the WCC to advise industry of planned industry activities that may interfere with ongoing whaling, or to suggest windows of opportunity (when whaling is not taking place) when industry activity may have minimal potential effects. Unfortunately, vessel activity not associated with the oil and gas industry (for example, commercial barge traffic) need not coordinate with the WCC in the same way, so that this is not a totally effective mechanism for the mitigation of all such potential effects. Other sorts of logistical support have been supplied at least in part by industry. These have included low-cost connex units (converted into seasonal cabins on Cross Island); a winch to help haul whales up at Cross Island; assistance with a steadier supply of gasoline; a generator system to supply electricity to the cabins during the whaling season; diesel fuel (for the winch and generator); water and other supplies; help with transporting the butchered whale to Nuiqsut; at least limited phone service for one or two crews; help with mobilization and demobilization; and the assurance of available emergency assistance. Alaska Clean Seas (ACS) is the industry's contractor for much of this OWA support, as a small part of its overall responsibilities (which are mainly logistical and/or related to oil spill response). BPXA and ConocoPhillips provide most of the funding for ACS, but BPXA bears the majority of OWA-related costs since ConocoPhillips has little or no offshore interests. The AEWC does pay for some of the services provided under the OWA, but the amount and exact services are not reported. Neither industry nor the AEWC discloses the financial terms of the OWA.

Preparations for whaling, in one form or another, take place during the entire year. This report focuses on the activities during the harvest season. The final preparation of boats and equipment happens in August, and a meeting of the NWCA is conducted to set a date for the start of the hunting effort and to review the rules and regulations. Labor Day is the normative date for whaling crews to go to Cross Island, but it is not unusual for individual crews to go out earlier, especially if Labor Day is "late." In 2003, one crew (with three boats) went out August 23. This was considered "early" by the other crews, but since whales were spotted by this crew two other crews went out August 29 (three boats), and the fourth crew on August 31 (three boats). Crews prefer to go out together or with multiple boats, for safety.

Once on Cross Island the focus is on whaling. Boats usually go scouting for whales on all possible days unless a whale was taken the prior day, in which case butchering usually has priority. When a whale is taken, it is towed to Cross Island, hauled up on the gravel beach, and butchered. Select parts of the whale are sent to Nuiqsut via whaling boat the same or the next day "to feed the village." The rest of the meat, muktuk, organs, and baleen is packed into plastic fish totes and transported to West Dock and then to Nuiqsut (most recently via ACS barge and air freight). What is left of the whale is disposed of in the "bone yard." Once the quota is taken or conditions threaten to prevent returning to Nuiqsut (formation of ice), the whalers clean up the island, pack, and leave. Most will return to Nuiqsut together. Captains who have taken whales that season will fly their flags. Whaling will usually be completed by mid- to late-September.

Nuiqsut whalers first used wood boats and relatively small motors. Although they remember these vessels with fondness, and long for the economy of those motors, they also remember that they were limited in terms of speed and towing capability. Currently Nuiqsut whalers all use aluminum or fiberglass boats, 17 to 24 feet long, with motors of 80 to 225 horsepower. It is possible that a 16-foot boat may be used as a whale boat on occasion, but it would not be considered a primary boat. A few boats have cabins, but most are open. Boats typically scout for whales with a complement of three or four people, although some boat crews are as small as two and as big as six. Although single boats do take whales on occasion, it is not encouraged and Nuiqsut boats almost always scout for whales in pairs, in case of mechanical break downs or other emergencies. Whaling crews with two or three boats are willing to whale on their own, but it is commonly agreed that five to seven boats is a preferable number to have available for whaling on a given day. More boats would be useful, and the availability of fewer boats decreases the efficiency, safety, and overall chance for success of the hunt.

Methodology

The data to be collected for this research will be discussed in terms of methods, with emphasis on the actual collection of descriptive information. In addition, it is important to address the issue of "hypothesis testing" in relation to the products of this research effort.

Hypothesis Testing

MMS explicitly required, as part of the proposal submission, the formulation of hypotheses related to potential changes in Cross Island subsistence whaling. These hypotheses can then eventually be tested using the information collected by this research effort. Two such hypotheses were formulated:

- H1: Subsistence whaling activity and behaviors in the vicinity of Cross Island are significantly changed by offshore oil developments at Northstar and/or Liberty.
- H2: General subsistence activities on/near Cross Island are significantly changed by oil and gas activities associated with Northstar and/or Liberty.

Hypotheses in the "null hypothesis" format are counterintuitive to at least some of the local research participants and perhaps to the general public at-large, although it will be necessary to express them in that form for quantitative testing. It was explicitly recognized that the annual reports would not be able to test these hypotheses. Such tests will require more data (longer time series) and significant effort devoted to analysis, and will be part of the cANIMIDA final report (after the 2006 field season).

In summary, the hypotheses have been formulated as examples of possible relationships that are testable after concrete empirical (and ideally quantitative) measures of Cross Island whaling have been compiled for a number of years. The hypotheses thus guide the practical methods of collecting and archiving the information, to ensure that they will be useful for testing these hypotheses (as well as others as they are developed).

Descriptive Data Categories

The primary goal of data collection is the compilation of quantified measures of subsistence whaling behavior. Emphasis has been placed on such measures as:

- Number of crews actively whaling
- Size and composition of crews
- Fluctuations in active crew size and composition over the whaling season
- Number of whales harvested
- Days spent whaling
- Days prevented from whaling (weather, equipment failure or repair, etc.)
- Days suitable for whaling when whaling did not occur
- Subsistence activities occurring other than whaling
- Location of whale sightings and whale harvest
- Location of whale searching
- Local weather and ice conditions

These measures are a mixture of descriptive characteristics suggested by MMS and factors derived from or related to the perceptions of whalers on how and why whale behavior has changed, requiring that whalers change their behavior in hunting whales. For instance, size and composition of crews are fundamental descriptive characteristics that must have some relationship with the availability of whales. They also depend on the alternative (non-Cross Island) activities available to the crew members, such as alternative subsistence activities, wage labor opportunities, education, and so on. Because of the focus on Cross Island activities, information on the "full" range of factors that may be affecting the data collected was thus not compiled, but the range of possibilities was generally elicited from whalers during discussions of topics such as crew composition or crew recruitment. In this sense, these generally descriptive measures are thus also characteristics identified by Nuiqsut whalers as potentially significant and variable measures from year-to-year. The locations of whale sightings, harvests, and general whale searching behavior are all important in the examination of whether whales can be found in the same locations every season, or if this changes from year-to-year. If the latter, what causes such shifts in location is important. Nuiqsut whalers have experienced such variation and have suggested a number of factors to account for it. This project develops information to examine these questions about variation and changes in Cross Island whaling behavior. For instance, this information will allow for a preliminary examination of "catch per unit effort" as well as factors associated with the distance whalers need to travel from Cross Island to whale.

Nuiqsut whalers generally agreed the suggested measures were significant and pertinent to the issues to be addressed. During the first field season (2001) Nuiqsut whalers also wanted to ensure that their more general perceptions and observations of whale behavior, and especially changes in whale behavior that had implications for hunting success or safety, were adequately noted. Such perceptions are also the most likely way for Nuiqsut whalers to contribute to future hypothesis formation and testing. Thus, information categories were added to ensure that whalers' perceptions and observations were noted on:
- Bowhead whale behavior in the Cross Island area, and indicated differences from past experience; and
- Changes in access or other issues related to the whale hunt, such as increased effort for the same (or reduced) harvest, increased risk, increased cost, and so on.

Consultation

Consultation for the third field season built on that for the first and second, described in the annual reports for 2001 and 2002, and the final report based on the results of those two years. In addition to periodic phone calls (primarily to the Native Village of Nuiqsut, the City of Nuiqsut, and various whaling captains in Nuiqsut; and the AEWC and IHLC in Barrow) and a presentation of project results at the MMS Information Transfer Meeting in Anchorage, 3/10/03-3/12/03, consultation efforts in 2003 consisted of:
- Trips to Barrow and Nuiqsut to discuss the project and to collect supplemental information:

- Barrow 3/13/03-3/15/03. This trip was primarily to present the results of the project at the MMS Information Transfer Meeting (3/14/03), but were used for short consultation visits to the AEWC and the IHLC as well.

- Nuiqsut 6/28/03-7/01/03, Barrow 7/01/03-7/02/03. In Nuiqsut, whaling captains and others reviewed draft versions of the final and annual reports. Preliminary arrangements for the 2003 field season were also confirmed. In Barrow the draft reports were also reviewed with AEWC staff, and arrangements made for the review of AEWC records at a later date.

- Barrow 7/09/03-7/11/03. Most of this trip was devoted to the examination of AEWC records pertaining to Nuiqsut (Cross Island) whaling.

- Barrow 7/15/03-7/18/03. This trip was scheduled at the invitation/suggestion of AEWC staff, as it would be an opportunity to talk with Nuiqsut and Kaktovik whaling captains about the project (they were in Barrow to discuss the Oil/Whalers Agreement). In addition, the trip was an opportunity to talk with IHLC staff to about potential resources that would be useful for the project. The IHLC tapes remain unprocessed, but are still of great potential benefit to the project. Some additional time was spent talking with AEWC staff and examining their records, and some further review of draft project documents.

- Nuiqsut and Cross Island 8/27/03-9/16/03. This was the 2003 field season

As in 2002, the field season arrangements became problematic as circumstances prevented some whaling captains from fielding crews in 2003. This again required hurried consultation, by phone, with the other Nuiqsut whaling captains. While four crews had plans to whale in 2003, this was essentially the same level of effort as for 2002. One of those crews had split off from one of the others. Two of the four crews already had complete crews and no room for additional people at their camps (other than for the already-arranged short-term visits from industry representatives interested in gaining some firsthand knowledge of Cross Island whaling). Luckily, one of the other captains invited the researcher to accompany his crew, and arrangements were made for him to accompany the Oyagak crew, with an anticipated date of departure for Cross Island during the first week of September, after Labor Day. As is described below, the Oyagak crew left Nuiqsut to go whaling on 8/29, while the first crew left 8/23.

Data Collection

The researcher left Anchorage for Nuiqsut (via Deadhorse) on August 27, to accompany the Oyagak crew to Cross Island. Nuiqsut whaling captains had advised that crews would probably not leave for Cross Island until after Labor Day, as this has been the case in the past and no one had expressed a desire to go earlier for 2003. As it happened, the Napageak crew left for Cross Island on August 23. They went scouting on the 8/25 and 8/27 and saw some small whales. This motivated the other crews to get ready as soon as possible, within reason. Weather prevented the Napageak crew from scouting for whales on 8/24, 8/26, and 8/28-8/31. This poor weather did not prevent other crews from traveling from Nuiqsut to Cross Island on 8/29 (Oyagak and Aqargiun crews) and 8/31 (Nukapigak crew). Most crews departed Cross Island 9/09, while the Napageak crew stayed an additional day and departed 9/10. The researcher was on Cross Island for most of the 2003 whaling season, and for all whale harvest activities.

Table 2 summarizes the whales struck by the Cross Island whalers in 2003 (a more detailed day-by-day presentation of daily whaling activity for the entire Cross Island whaling season is presented in Table 5 later in this report). On September 1st, the Aqargiun struck and landed a whale. This whaling captain had taken three whales in 2002 for the Nukapigak crew, but had decided to start his own crew in 2003. The Aqargiun crew struck and landed their second whale on the 5th. The Napageak crew also struck and landed a whale on the 5th. The Napageak crew struck and landed their second whale on the 6th. This completed the quota for Nuiqsut.

Three types of data were collected during the 2003 field season, as discussed above. These are GPS information; systematic observations of quantifiable measurements of various components of subsistence whaling activity; and whalers' observations on whale behavior (and especially changes in such behavior). This last sort of information is often accompanied by perceptions of possible causes for such changes and the implications such changes may have for subsistence whaling activities.

Table 2: Summary Characteristics[1] of Whales Struck Near Cross Island, 2003

Date	Time Struck	Length	Sex	Whale ID	Miles from Cross Island	Bearing from Cross Island	Notes[2]
9/01/03	12:55 PM	26'1"	M	03N1	5.2 mi.	15° true	Struck and Landed Aqargiun crew
9/05/03	7:32 AM	27'9"	F	03N2	9.7 mi.	89° true	Struck and landed Aqargiun crew
9/05/03	8:06 AM	41'9"	M	03N3	12.2 mi.	77° true	Struck and landed, first struck with harpoon and float (no bomb) Napageak crew
9/06/03	8:18 PM	39'1"	M	03N4	10.1 mi	44° true	Struck and landed Napageak crew

[1]All characteristics are from direct observations or GPS records made on the day of the activity, other than the WhaleID number. WhaleID numbers are assigned by the North Slope Borough Department of Wildlife Management (NSB DW). Times are approximate and are derived from the recorded GPS tracks and/or radio logs, combined with whalers' accounts, as are the distances from Cross Island.
[2]Whales were first struck with a harpoon (armed with a bomb) with an attached float, unless otherwise noted. Exceptions are rare.

GPS Data

All whalers participating in the research in 2003 had participated in the research in previous years. Although 2003 was the first year for the Aqargiun crew as a separate crew, the captain had operated one of the Nukapigak boats in previous years and in 2002 had taken three whales for his captain. In any event, all crews whaling in 2003 were reasonably familiar with the goals and methods of the project, and in using a GPS unit. All crews but one (Aqargiun) had been issued GPS units in 2001 and/or 2002, but several required an additional unit either because of using an additional boat or the loss of old units. Most new GPS units were Garmin GPS72s, as they have more and better features than the Garmin GPS12 units, although they require another short training session (one whaler did request a replacement GPS12). Whalers were again instructed to record the locations of whale strikes, whale kills, or other subsistence activities or observations. Most boats had at least one crew member familiar with GPS units, and most boats used them as a matter of course. GPS tracks were recovered for most scouting trips (96 percent for the period when the researcher was on Cross Island, 88 percent overall).

All crews were instructed to keep the "tracking" feature on, which recorded the path the boat traveled each time it went out. However, as in previous years, these tracks were sometimes incomplete or composed of several separate tracks, due to the unit losing its positional fix. Possible causes included periods of inadequate satellite coverage/availability or the unit being turned off. All boats were provided with a power cord so that the GPS units could be operated from the boat's electrical system, so that depleted batteries were not the problem they had been in 2001. Also, all boats were provided with a boat-mounted holder for the GPS unit, so that the units would be readily available, secure, and not be mistakenly shielded from satellite signals due to being put in a pocket. Some units were forgotten or simply not turned on for some trips, and at times satellite coverage was spotty. Whalers were instructed how to mark points, and told to mark the points where whales were seen. Whalers were also asked to mark other events such as "blows," other animals (polar bears, seals, and so on) and key points in their trip (ice in an otherwise iceless trip, place where weather conditions change, and so on). Positions where whales were seen, struck, or killed were marked by a number of crews, but were seldom if ever labeled and so required additional discussion with the crew and additional processing of the "track" file. Fewer points were marked in 2003 than in previous years, but fewer days were spent scouting for whales as well. In any event, the process of increasing the incidence of marking significant points will require steady attention and constant encouragement.

The researcher visited each crew that had gone out for the day after they came back, in order to download the information from their GPS unit into his laptop computer. This ensured that the GPS units were always available to the crews should they decide to go out at short notice. This procedure also enabled the crews to immediately see where they had been that day with the mapping software, and allowed the crew an opportunity to discuss their trip with the researcher while it was very fresh in their minds. The utility of this information, as concretely represented on the mapped tracks displayed by the computer, was immediately obvious to the whalers and appeared to be one reason for the high degree of participation. An example of the combined tracks for one day of scouting can be seen in Figure 2. Figures for all such tracks are included in electronic appendix A on the CD-ROM attached to this report. The MMS Alaska OCS Region holds the processed GPS data files.

Hunters were also asked to report other subsistence efforts and results, in terms of time spent, species, number, and location in terms of GPS coordinates. Little such activity was reported.

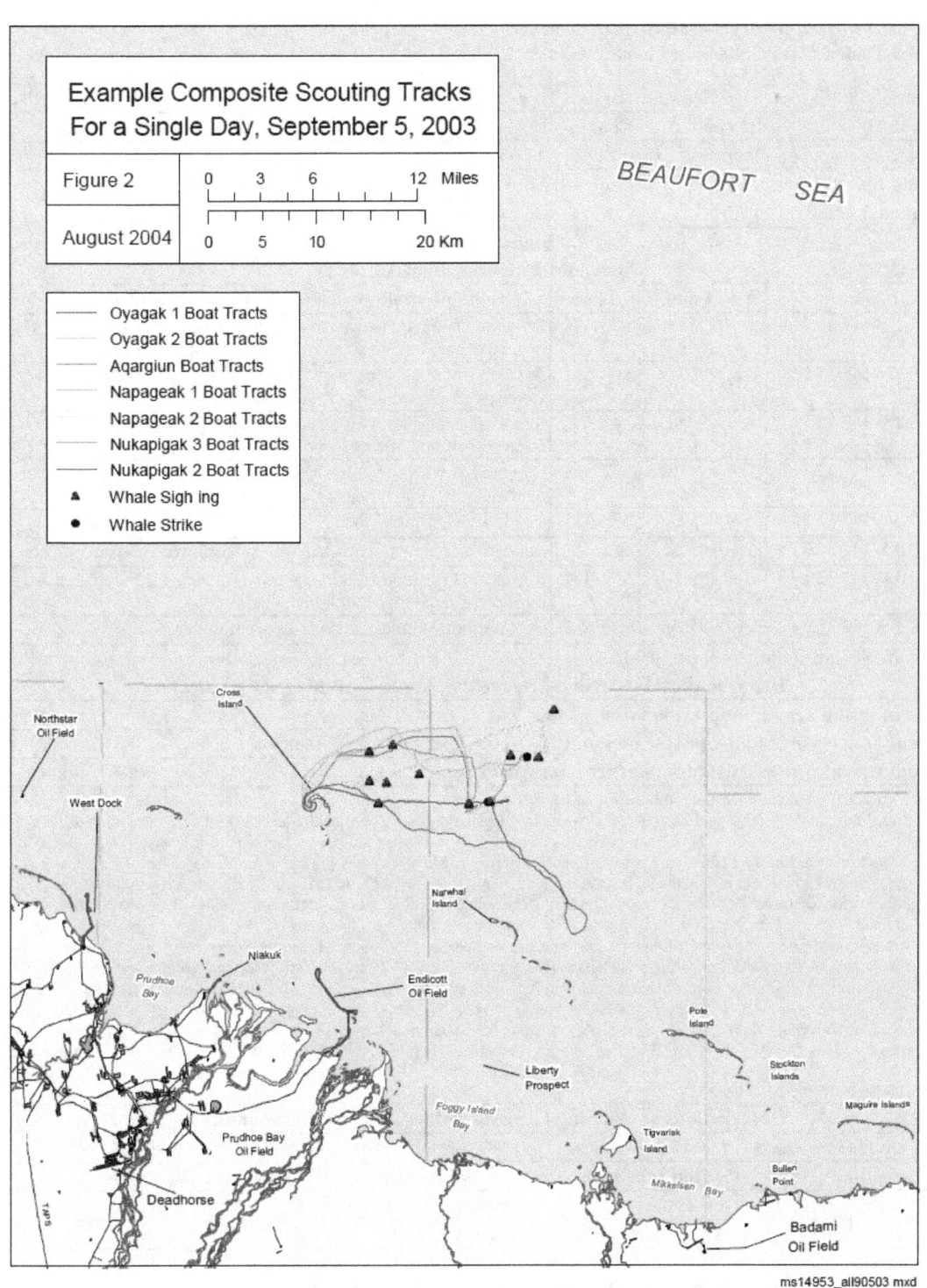

Example Composite Scouting Tracks For a Single Day, September 5, 2003

Figure 2	0 3 6 12 Miles
August 2004	0 5 10 20 Km

BEAUFORT SEA

——— Oyagak 1 Boat Tracts
——— Oyagak 2 Boat Tracts
——— Aqargiun Boat Tracts
——— Napageak 1 Boat Tracts
——— Napageak 2 Boat Tracts
——— Nukapigak 3 Boat Tracts
——— Nukapigak 2 Boat Tracts
▲   Whale Sigh ing
●   Whale Strike

Beaufort Sea

Northstar Oil Field
Cross Island
West Dock
Narwhal Island
Niakuk
Prudhoe Bay
Endicott Oil Field
Pole Island
Stockton Islands
Liberty Prospect
Foggy Island Bay
Maguire Islands
Prudhoe Bay Oil Field
Tigvariak Island
Mikkelsen Bay
Bullen Point
Deadhorse
Badami Oil Field

ms14953_all90503.mxd

Daily boat report forms were used to capture this GPS information. Forms for all days for all boats are included in Appendix A. Table 3 below presents an example of the information collected for one of the boat tracks included in Figure 2 above. The form for the 2003 field

Table 3: Example Daily Boat Report Form
ANIMIDA Task 4 Data Collection Form, 2003   **Use one form for each vessel/day**

Date: 09/05/03   **Crew:** Aqargiun   **GPS Type:** Garmin 12

Vessel	Type	Length	HP Motor	# crew aboard/notes
IAN	Fiberglass	20'	Yamaha 125 HP	4

Whaling today? Yes   **If not, why not?** _____

Time departed: 6:06 AM   **Time returned:** 11:03 AM

4 hours 57 minutes

Waypoints or Coordinates noted

Lat/Long	Way Point #	Time	Notes (if whale - # of animals, direction of travel, behavior)
N70 32 17.7 W147 46 46.9	ian_090503a	6:26 AM	Position when IAN slowed to look for whales because NAP2 had seen one. NAP2 was to the south of IAN boat somewhat more than 1 mile.
N70 31 39.7 W147 35 02.0	ian_090503b	7:07 AM	Position where IAN resumed "traveling" speed – possibly because they were called to a whale NAP2 was following.
N70 29 29.2 W147 35 21.6	IAN_090503c	7:13 AM	Reported as position IAN struck the whale. It is more consistent with radio reports and other accounts that this is a sighting waypoint.
N70 29 34.4 W147 32 34.3	IAN_090503d	7:32 AM	Reported as where IAN bat had to turn around 180 degrees. More consistent that this is where the whale was first struck.
N70 29 39.8 W147 32 28.0	ian_090503e	7:38 AM	Likely IAN position when NAP2 put in 2nd darting gun bomb
N70 29 40.0 W147 32 25.4	ian_090503f	7:52 AM	Likely IAN position when IAN killed whale with shoulder gun bomb
N70 29 37.3 W147 32 17.7	IAN_090503g	8:02 AM	Reported as position IAN had to turn around again. More consistent as location of radio report of killed whale
N70 29 28.1 W147 31 34.2	ian_090503h	8:20 AM	IAN position at time of reported start of tow

Length of 27'9", tail flukes 8'5", slit of 11"

Describe the day's activity (traveling, hours searching for whales)

Direction of initial search (and explanation):	North, then NE and east
Time spent actively scouting/# people looking:	6:06-7:32 AM – 86 minutes
Time spent in travel/tow/assistance to other boats/on "break":	8:20-11:03 AM – 2 hours 43 minutes

Notes: From account of crews and examinations of tracks

Headed out north, then NE and east. BO boats were in the general area, as was NAP2 and NAP3 (NAP1 stayed pretty much to the north, NUK boats went SE). NAP2 saw a whale or a blow and all boats slowed to scout more intensively (ian_090503a). They evidently kept at this until NAP2 called them to help with the whale NAP2 was following (all boats converged on NAP2 position). Several boats had chances at this whale. It was reported to have come up twice by NAP2 and a third time by the BO boats. BO2 lined up for a shot when another boat was reported to spook the whale by going over its trail of air bubbles. The whale then came up near BO2 and NAP2 but not in a position for a shot, and when it dove it changed directions by 180 degrees. Thus it came up in back of them and they were going in the wrong direction to chase it, whereas IAN was headed in the same direction as the whale. Thus IAN actually had the first good shot at this whale and made the strike. All other boats then left to resume scouting except for NAP2, which assisted in the kill – put in a second darting gun bomb about 5 minutes after the first strike (whale went down a little after 1st strike, then came up). IAN killed the whale with a final shoulder gun bomb (about 15 or 20 minutes later – whale stayed down that long). See waypoints above. NAP2 boat left to resume scouting when the NUK boats arrived in the area (at about 7:45 AM) and IAN and NUK boats towed the IAN whale to Cross Island and started butchering. TOT 4:57, total distance 34.1 miles, FDFCI 11.3 miles. Whale was initially thought to be female, may be male. 27'9", tail flukes 8'5", slit of 11". Strike 9.7 MFCI, kill 10.1 to 10.5 MFCI [some uncertainty on strike location]

Observations of Whaling Crew - weather, sea state, ice-conditions

Fog or clouds	clouds	Weather notes:	Trying to snow, temperature in the 30s; BP peaks at 3PM @ 29.8 and then falls
Wind Direction:	SW	**Wind speed and other notes:**	Varies – 0 to 18 mph – see WF
% Ice Coverage:	0	**Ice Type:**	**Other Notes:**
Wave Height:		**Other notes on sea conditions:**	
Other pertinent notes:	See weather station file		

Note: Cross Island weather observations are compiled in a separate file (weather station + observer)

Engaged in any other subsistence activities? No   **If yes, describe below**

Butchered own whale, helped with NAP2 whale.

GPS track? Yes **GPS File Name:** IAN_090503.mps

If not, why not?

season was modified from that for previous years, based on suggestions from the Scientific Review Board. A list of acronyms and abbreviations used in provided on page ix.

The information used in the Table 3 example was not chosen at random, but rather because it demonstrates some of the difficulties presented in the waypoint information reported in this (and previous) documents. Although instructed to mark waypoints whenever whales are spotted or where significant events take place, no crew in fact can do so, for a variety of reasons. Whaling events happen so quickly that crew members are fully occupied with their duties and sometimes cannot divert their attention to mark a point (or perhaps even remember to do so). When points are marked, crews seldom take the time to assign them names, so that they are designated with "default" numbers. When waypoints are marked, they do not necessarily represent the same thing. Waypoints indicating where a whale was struck or killed for the most part represent the immediate area where that event took place. Those indicating a whale sighting are less precise, showing the position of a boat when a whale was sighted. It may indicate a whale seen a short distance away, or the "blow" of a whale seen in the distance (up to 2 or 3 miles away). Also, a waypoint may represent one whale or multiple whales.

Since most crews will discuss most of their trips with the researcher, it has been possible to collect more waypoint information that is present in the GPS data files, but with a further loss of precision. Crews remember how many whales they have seen on a trip, and generally where they were. When looking at the mapped tracks of their trip they are able to identify where they saw whales, so that an approximate waypoint can be generated. In most cases, sighting locations are associated with changes in a boat's direction. Such "generated" waypoints are differentiated from those actually marked by crews by using lowercase letters in their labels.

Some marked waypoints are also somewhat ambiguous in meaning, however, since the crew may assign one meaning or memory to a point ("strike") when in fact it may have another ("sighting"). That is, especially when whales are harvested, whalers may misidentify the waypoints that they do mark. Given that crew members have little attention to spare in this situation, and that the waypoints themselves are usually only numbered, and that the crew may not remember exactly how many waypoints were marked (or if all attempts to mark points actually succeeded), such confusion can be expected. However, since whalers communicate with each other, the WCC, and sometimes their Cross Island base station, by radio it is often possible to note when significant events take place by what is said on the radio and noting the time. When compared to the date stamps on waypoints these notes can then aid in the interpretation of what the waypoints actually represent. It should also be noted that the researcher is also a potential source of confusion, in that his understanding of a crew's description of their trip activities and events may in fact be in error – the researcher may misinterpret what the crew tells him. The data as presented is the result of comparative cross-checks using the information obtained from all sources (GPS, crew accounts, radio notes).

All of these factors are evident in the information presented in Table 3. Some waypoints are generated based on what was heard on the radio and/or reported by the crew. Some marked waypoints, reported as representing one event, are concluded to probably represent another. These ambiguities of meaning influence the way in which the points can be used but not to the extent that they do not have meaning. Whale sighting waypoints can not be interpreted as point locations. Whale strike and kill locations can generally be interpreted as point locations, but not necessarily precise point locations. Boats are always moving and waypoints are seldom if ever marked at the precise time that a strike is made or a whale is killed.

Systematic Observations

Systematic observations were transferred to standardized recording forms (daily boat report forms). These observations are the basis for the summary tables that appear in the "Results" section, as well as the completed daily vessel activity forms. From these records it is possible to make a basic "census" of the crews on the island, and to track changes as people came to Cross Island and left. In addition, notes were made on which crews went out on each day. In most cases it was possible to note who went out in each boat. From these basic observations can be derived some of the most basic measures of subsistence whaling activity – number of active crews (and boats), size and composition of crews, fluctuations in crew size and composition, and days spent whaling. The GPS data provide systematic locational information for whaling activities. This information also was recorded on the daily boat report forms. Examples of the daily boat report forms appear below as Tables 3 and 4. The complete series of forms is included as Appendix A. A list of the acronyms and abbreviations used in these tables (and elsewhere in the report) is provided on page ix.

In addition, very basic weather observations were made (temperature, wind direction and strength, degree of fogginess or clarity, barometric pressure). A weather station was installed on Cross Island, with a remote data logger to record the information. The data logger functioned for the period 8/30 (3:35 PM) through 9/09 (10:33 AM), with readings every five minutes for temperature (outdoor and indoor), wind speed, wind direction, barometric pressure, and relative humidity (file CI2003WF.xls, also included as Appendix B). Good readings for outdoor temperature and relative humidity only started 8/31 at 12:09 AM, due to problems between that sensor and the data logger. Any weather observations prior to 8/30 (the researcher's first full day on Cross Island) are based on reports from the Napageak crew.

Since January 1, 2001 MMS has maintained a weather station at Endicott, which is close enough to Cross Island to be pertinent. The datalog is available at **www.resdat.com/mms**. This is another potential data set of interest for the analysis of the whaling data (MMS also maintains weather stations at Northstar, Badami, Milne Point, and Cottle Island). Other potential sources of weather information and whaling activities are the communications logs of the Whaling Communications Center. Since the researcher could not go out in the boat while they scouted for whales, he had little ability to judge the degree of ice cover, although the Nuiqsut whalers did report their observations in a general way. There was little ice cover in 2003, with ice observations being noted on the daily boat report forms. Information on ice cover may be obtainable from remote sensing sources or the MMS aerial bowhead survey.

Whalers' Observations

Whalers would sometimes make observations on whale behavior or give their thoughts on how and why whale behavior in the Cross Island area was different in 2003 than it had been in the past, and especially in 2001 and 2002. Much of this was recorded in the daily fieldnotes. Much is of limited immediate relevance to the central aims of this project. A summary of the most pertinent information is included in the "Results" section.

Results

Results are discussed in this section in terms of the quantitative observations designed as measures of subsistence whaling activity and the less quantifiable observations and perceptions of Nuiqsut whalers about whale behavior in 2003 as compared to previous years.

Quantitative Measures

A summary of basic information, based on Table 4 and Figure 3 below, address the primary descriptive characteristics of Cross Island subsistence whaling of most concern for MMS. In 2003, four crews from Nuiqsut whaled from Cross Island. Two crews used three boats each for whaling, and a fourth boat for logistical support. The third crew used two boats, and the fourth crew used one boat. Thus nine boats were used for whaling, and two more for support.

The size and composition of the crews differed from that of 2001 and 2002, primarily because of the "one boat" crew. The captain of this crew had previously whaled with another crew – 2003 was his first year as a registered whaling captain. His crew consisted primarily of four adult males (a brother and a nephew among them). Three younger (adolescent) males, all of them sons of the captain, joined the crew for the last three days of the season (after the quota had been harvested). A non-Inupiat male was a guest of this crew for three days in the middle of the season. The other three crews arrived at Cross Island with seven to nine members, with most being adult or adolescent males (one was an 8th grader, two were female adults). One of these crews had no changes during the season, while the two others each gained two members toward the end of the season, and one lost a member for health reasons. There were no "visitors" from Nuiqsut to help butcher the whales or for non-whaling activities in 2003.

Crew Characteristics

All crews had a majority of adult members, but differed in the age of the youngest member and the ratio of older to younger members. Two crews had no members younger than a high school graduate (19 or 20), one was composed of adults and one 8th grader, and the fourth whaled only with adult males, but added 3 adolescent males once the harvest was complete. Two of the four crews were composed of about equal numbers of "mature adults" (over the age of 25) and "young adults" (age 18-25). One crew was composed of six adult males and an 8th grader. The fourth crew was the composed of four adult males, and once the quota was harvested, 3 young adults/adolescents. Kinship and kin relations were clearly important for the composition of all four crews, but differed in the way they were expressed in each crew. One crew was composed of more "immediate" family, with in-laws perhaps more important for another, and a combination of kinship and friendship relationships important for the other two crews.

Crews also differed in the number of people who actually manned the boat while whaling (and manned is the proper term on Cross Island, as only two of the total crew members were women). Generally, female crew members only went in the boat when the captain deemed there was space available – about 50 percent of the time in 2003. A whaling boat normally requires a minimum of three crew members – a driver, a harpooner, and a person in charge of the float – although boats will sometimes go out with only two crew members. A fourth crew member is sometimes assigned to the shoulder gun. Depending on conditions and intuition, a whaling captain may desire to take as few crew members as possible (to have a light, fast boat) or as many extra as possible (to have as many eyes watching for whales as possible).

In 2003, two boats most commonly went out with only two crew members. One was the boat that had exhibited this pattern in 2002, while another used two only crew members for other reasons. This boat had been manned with 3 or more crew members in previous years when it had a 130 horsepower motor. However, in 2003 it had an 80 horsepower motor. In addition, this crew as a whole was relatively smaller than it had been in past years. That is, there were few or no "excess" crew members who were not needed to man the boats while scouting. This was generally true for all crews – few had more than one crew member more than the number normally expected to go out scouting for whales. There were also fewer "young" crew members than in previous years, with only one student included on one crew. Thus it is not surprising that the size of boat crews was smaller than in previous years, ranging from 2 to 4 crew members except for two days for one crew, when they had mechanical problems on one of their principal boats. On those days their boat crew size was 5 or 6 instead of 4 (Table 4).

Whaling Days

During the whaling season there were 7 days when Nuiqsut whalers were documented to go out scouting for whales. Two of these days were before the researcher reached Cross Island, but at least a partial track was collected for each day on which scouting occurred. These are the shaded cells in Table 4 – dark cells are those scouting trips for which no GPS track is available, while light cells represent scouting trips for which GPS tracks were collected. Only one crew experienced significant mechanical problems in 2003 – but still had 2 boats to use for scouting and 1 for logistical support (and the fourth boat did scout one day). The other three crews used a total of six boats for scouting – three for one crew, two for another, and one for the third. Thus, of the nine primary whaling boats, eight had the opportunity to whale every day that conditions were appropriate while they were at Cross Island.

The 2003 Cross Island whaling season was 19 days (from the arrival of the first crew to the departure of the last). Crews spent four days on Cross Island for butchering, clean up activities, packing, and travel after completing their quota with the harvest of the fourth whale. Of the 15 days on which scouting for whales would have been possible, 1 was devoted to travel to Cross Island. Scouting for whales occurred on 7 of these days, although for one of these days (9/03/03) conditions were so marginal that only one crew went out, and they did not stay out long. Weather prevented any scouting activity on the other 7 days. In general, although the 2003 whaling season was effectively only 15 days, the weather was poor. No

Table 4: Summary of Boat Activity, Cross Island Whaling, 2003

DATE	Napageak1 Crew	Napageak1 Trip	Napageak2 Crew	Napageak2 Trip	Napageak3 Crew	Napageak3 Trip	Oyagak1 Crew	Oyagak1 Trip	Oyagak2 Crew	Oyagak2 Trip	Aqargiun Crew	Aqargiun Trip	Nukapigak1 Crew	Nukapigak1 Trip	Nukapigak2 Crew	Nukapigak2 Trip	Nukapigak3 Crew	Nukapigak3 Trip	Notes
8/23/04		To CI/3		To CI/3		To CI/3	Still in Nuiqsut						Still in Nuiqsut						NAP crew to CI – 9 members
8/24/04			Weather																9 people on CI
8/25/04	UNK	UNK	UNK	UNK	UNK	UNK													9 people on CI, 9 scouting
8/26/04			Weather																9 people on CI
8/27/04	UNK	2:45	UNK	2:45	UNK	5:52*													9 people on CI, 9 scouting
8/28/04			Weather																9 people on CI
8/29/04								To CI/3		To CI/4		To CI/4							BO and IAN crews to CI – 7/4; 20 people on CI (2 leave late)
8/30/04									Weather										18 people on CI
8/31/04														To CI/3	To CI/2	To CI/2	To CI/2		NUK crew to CI – 7 members; 25 people on CI
9/01/04	3	5:07	3	4:51	To WD/3	Back w/4	2	3:42	4	3:33	4	4:15	Mechanical		4 or 5	3:23	Crew on NUK2		26 people on CI, 6 boats w/21 people out, IAN 1st whale
9/02/04	3	4:54*	2	1:09	3/2	5:26*	2	4:34*	3/4	4:33*	4	Butchering	6	4:02	Crew on NUK1		Crew on NUK1		ACS barge in w/1 whaler, 27 people on CI, 6 boats w/20
9/03/04	Weather														4	2:46	3	2:47	ACS barge in w/1, 28 people on CI, 2 boats w/7 whale
9/04/04													Weather						28 people on CI
9/05/04	3	8:56	3	8:56	2	8:54	2	9:06	3	9:06	4	4:57	Mechanical		4	5:16	3	5:16	NUK4 boat to CI, 30 people on CI. 8 boats w/23 people whale. IAN 2nd whale, NAP 1st whale.
9/06/04	Stayed on Shore		3	4:18		To NQT/3	3	6:04	2	6:09	To	NQT/UNK			2	6:31	2	6:31	ACS barge takes 1 away, 29 people on CI. 6 boats w/16 whale. NAP 2nd whale. 2 boats to NQT.
9/07/04	Quota filled, butchering, preparing to pack and return to Nuiqsut		To CI and back to NQT/2		To CI and back to NQT/2		Quota filled, butchering, preparing to pack and return to Nuiqsut				To CI/UNK		Quota filled, butchering, preparing to pack and return to Nuiqsut						33 people on CI. NAP4 boat to CI. ACS barge takes 1 away. 1 boat to CI & back to CI w/3
9/08/04	Divide crew shares				In NQT		Preparing to return to Nuiqsut						Preparing to return to Nuiqsut						29 people on CI
9/09/04	Final chores to cleanup and pack to return to NQT		To CI/2, help with chores		To CI/2, help with chores		To NQT/3		To NQT/3		To NQT/4		To NQT/2 or 3		To NQT/3		To NQT/2		31 people on CI. 1 boat back to CI w/2. 7 boats to NQT.
9/10/04	To NQT/3**		To NQT/2**		To NQT/2**		In Nuiqsut						In Nuiqsut						9 people on CI. Leave on 4 boats to NQT.

Notes on Table 3

See text for discussion of other vessel activity, or qualifications on entries above. "UNK" indicates that the information is not available.

Napageak4 and Nukapigak4 are not included in this table in order to keep it on one page. Both were at Cross Island for only a limited time (4 or 5 days). NAP4 was strictly a support boat, while NUK4 went scouting on one day (09/0/603) – TOT 6:31, crew of 2, GPS track collected.

"Weather" indicates that conditions were deemed by whalers to be too marginal for productive scouting. See discussion in text.

Travel days (not primarily devoted to scouting for whales) indicated by "to" or "from" with an indication of the number on board. An "or" indicates uncertainty in this number or a change during the trip. For whale scouting days, "Crew" is the number of people that went out on a given boat. "Trip" is the duration (in hours:minutes) for a daily trip. On days whales are harvested, see individual daily boat reports for duration of scouting versus duration of tow.

Indicates two scouting trips on this day – combined time. On 9/02, the first trip for these boats was in marginal weather and was relatively short. NAP2 only went out in "marginal" weather in the morning. NUK1 during calmer weather later in the day.

SHADED cells: boats potentially whaling

GPS Track NOT Collected

GPS Track Collected

Some GPS tracks are partial, some "non-whaling GPS tracks were collected (see daily boat report forms)

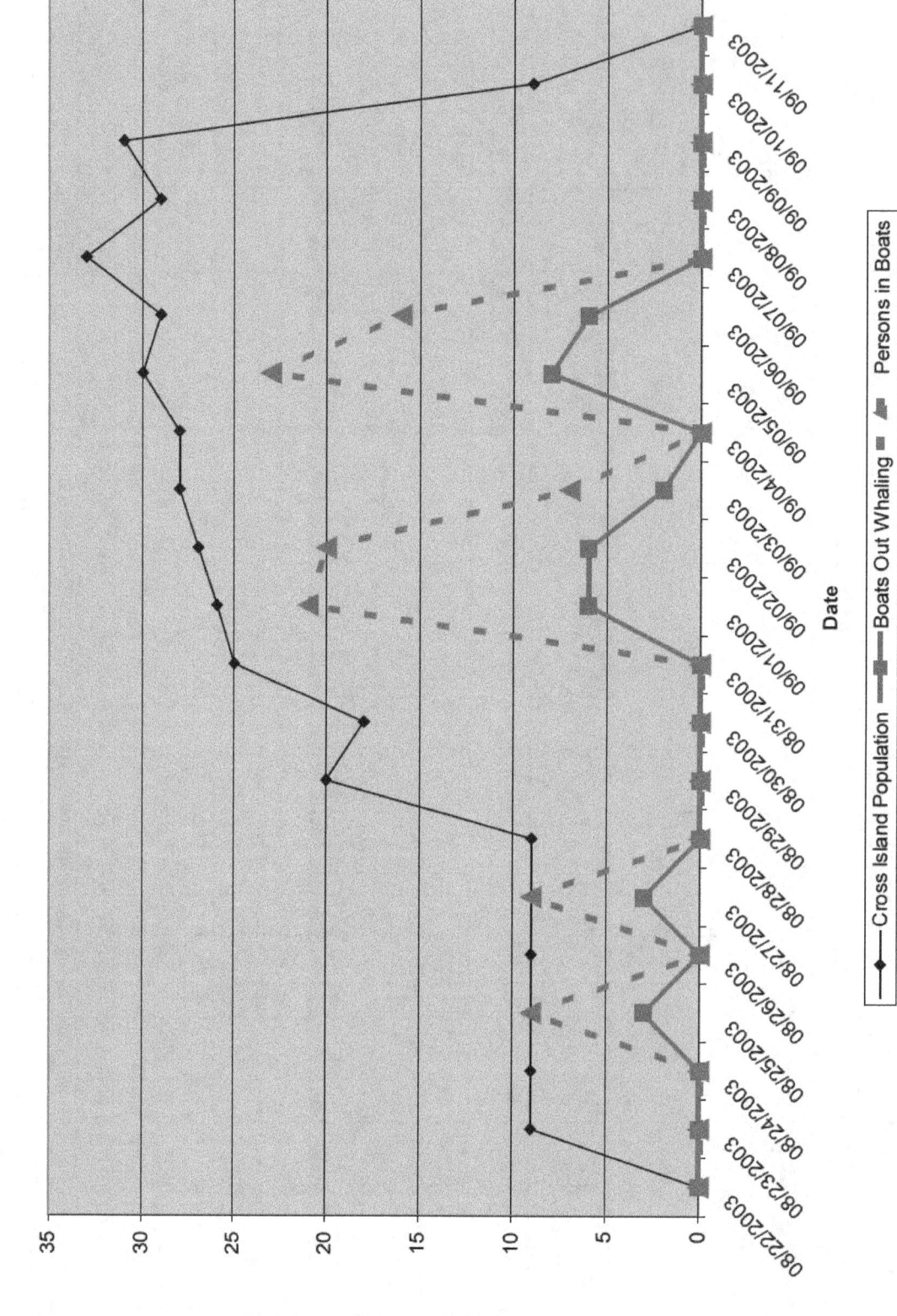

Figure 3: Cross Island Population, 2003

Number (People or Boats)

Date

— Cross Island Population ■ Boats Out Whaling ▲ Persons in Boats

ANIMIDA Task Order 004   page   20   2003 Annual Report, 05/07/05

scouting could occur 8/28/04-8/31/04, although the weather did not prevent boats from traveling from Nuiqsut to Cross Island. Even on days when scouting took place, conditions were quite variable throughout the day and sometimes only a few hours were actually suitable for scouting.

The first whale was taken 9/01/03 (struck about 12:55 PM, killed about 1:48 PM). Even though butchering was not complete by the next day, the successful captain gave his permission for the other crews to go out scouting, once conditions became favorable in the evening of 9/02/03 when the wind calmed down. However, no whale was taken 9/02/03, and weather (wind and high seas) prevented scouting for whales on the next two days. When conditions were again favorable, on 9/05/03, a small whale was taken early in the day (struck 7:32 AM, killed about 7:52 to 8:00 AM). Since two crews could tow and start to butcher this whale, and conditions were still good, the decision was made for the two other crews to try for a second small whale. A second whale was taken (struck between 8:00 and 8:24 AM, killed about 10:05 AM). Conditions were marginal for most of the following day, but became calm in the evening. Since butchering had progressed to the point where most of the common work was done, some crews were allowed to resume scouting. This decision was made in order to take advantage of whatever periods of good scouting conditions there were. The fear was that if they did not go out scouting, conditions might not be as good as this for several more days. The fourth whale was taken about 8:18 PM – the third whale in two days – to complete the 2003 Nuiqsut quota.

The weather factors that seem to affect when Nuiqsut whalers scout for whales appear to be barometric pressure and wind speed (and to some extent direction). Barometric pressure changes relatively slowly, and whalers often scout when it is in transition, but good scouting conditions tend to correspond with high barometric pressure or times of transition (Figure 4). Nuiqsut whalers do not observe barometric pressure directly – or, at least did not do so until the start of this research and the appearance of a weather station on Cross Island. If the barometric pressure trend is available, whalers will take it into account when deciding whether to scout for whales or not. Since it is at best a rough predictive tool, however, and whalers know from experience that a (relatively brief – up to several hours) period of good scouting conditions can occur when the wind shifts directions. Nuiqsut whalers thus rely much more on their direct observations of the wind and their experience as to what the future wind conditions will likely be. The wind conditions for the 2003 Cross Island whaling season are displayed in Figure 5, with more detail for the days on which scouting occurred (9/01-9/02 and 9/05-9/06). It can easily be seen that scouting activities correspond with periods of lower wind speeds. It should be noted that conditions on Cross Island are not necessarily the same as experienced when scouting for whales, but the general trends are often the same (complete weather file in electronic appendix).

In 2003 Scouting for whales occurred on 7 separate days, with a total of 34 boat-days devoted to this activity (each boat scouting for any amount of time on any given day counts as 1 boat-day). The median number of boats scouting on each of these 7 days was 5, with the average being 4.86. The average boat crew (for the 28 trips for which it is known) was 2.86 people, with a range of 2 to 6 people. Whales were struck an average of 9.3 miles from Cross Island (closer than for either 2001 or 2002). An average scouting trip (for the 31 trips for which it is known) lasted 5 hours, 15 minutes, with a median of 4 hours, 57 minutes. The range was 1 hours, 9 minutes to 9 hours, 6 minutes. The total effort on the water was about 163 boat-hours with 3 unknown days). These time estimates include as components:

Figure 4: Barometric Pressure During the 2003 Cross Island Whaling Season

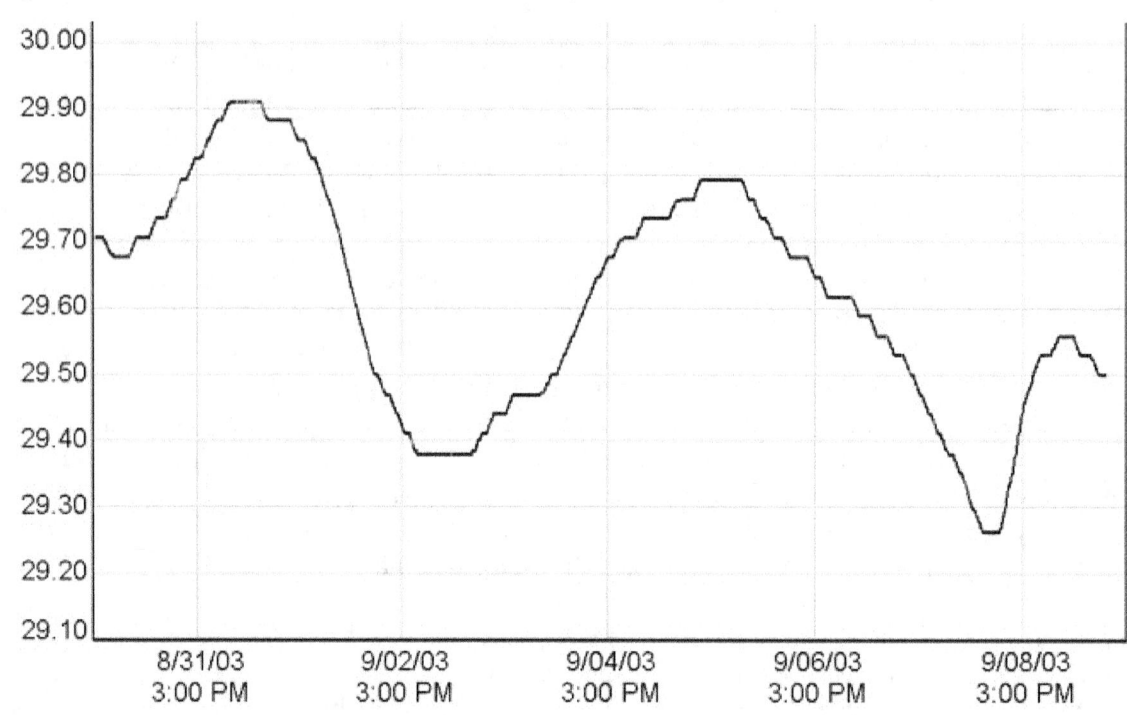

- transit time (at high speed en route to a search area or on the way back to Cross Island)
- scouting time (when actually looking for whales)
- following and chasing time (after finding a whale)
- towing time (after killing a whale)
- other miscellaneous activities (assistance to other boats, mechanical breakdown, rest breaks, and so on).

A detailed breakout of such separate activities is not easily done, although it is possible through close analysis of the GPS track information. Rough breakouts could be compiled with a reasonable level of effort. More exact accounting would require a high level of effort. By any measure, however, the time spent on the water in 2003 was much less than in 2001 or 2002.

Some generalizations about the factors influencing decisions to go whaling are possible, although no systematic model can yet be developed. If the weather is suitable for successful scouting of whales (slight or no wind, slight or no chop, good visibility), all boats physically able to whale will go out. Some captains will go out in more marginal weather than others, and such decisions are quite situational in nature. A crew that has not been out recently seems more likely to go out in marginal weather than those crews that have been out more recently. Crews that have not harvested whales seem more likely to go out whaling than those crews that have landed whales. A captain may call a "rest day" for a crew that has been working hard, especially if conditions are marginal. Trips on days with marginal weather conditions tend to be shorter than

Figure 5: Wind Speed and Direction Graphs for the 2003 Cross Island Whaling Season

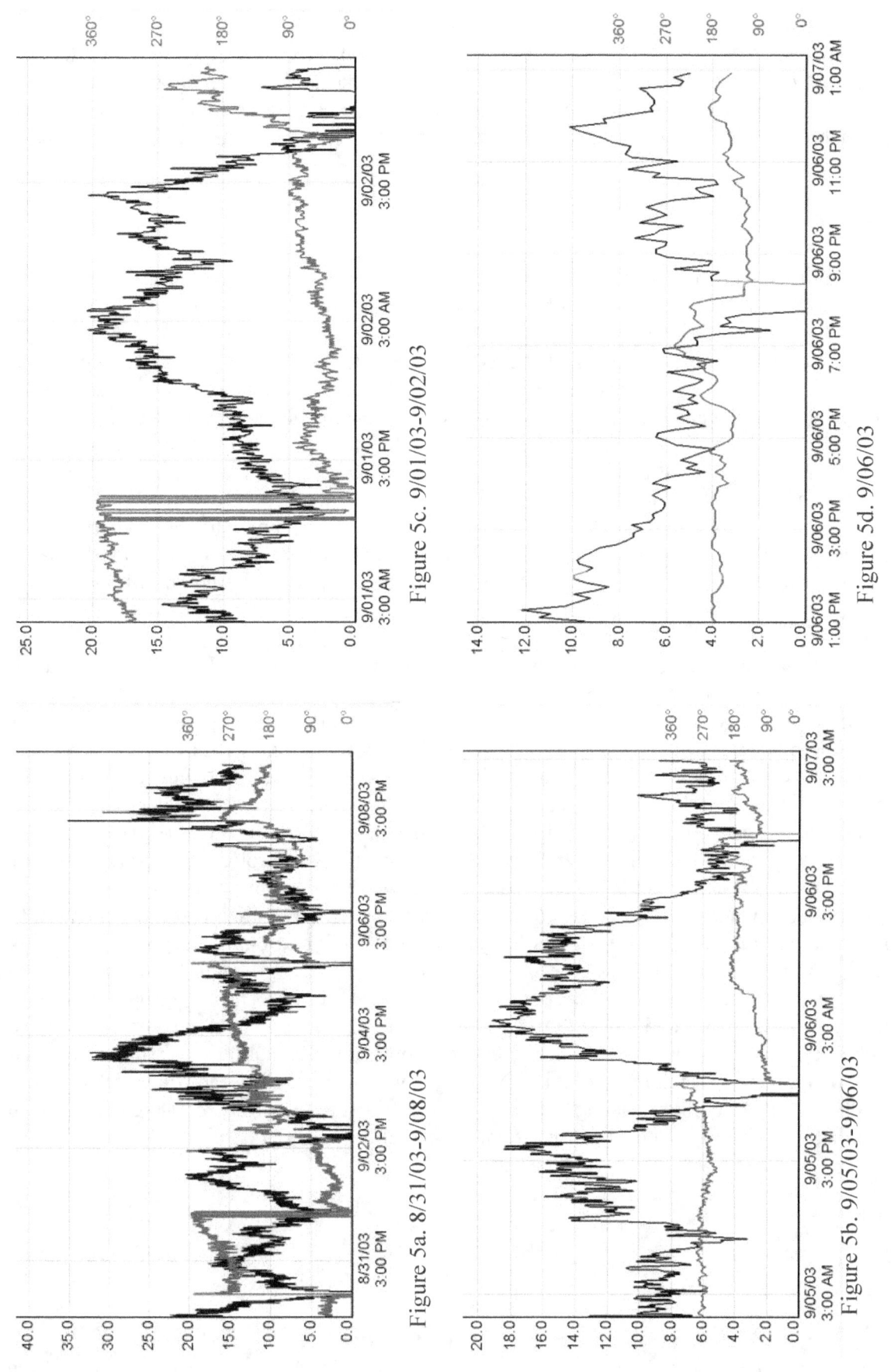

Figure 5a. 8/31/03-9/08/03

Figure 5b. 9/05/03-9/06/03

Figure 5c. 9/01/03-9/02/03

Figure 5d. 9/06/03

on days with better weather. After the harvest of a whale the butchering must reach a well-defined point before whaling can resume. For Nuiqsut whalers this is generally the next day for crews other than that which took the whale, and is often the next day for that crew as well. Crews go whaling in suitable weather and any deviation from that pattern has a specific explanation.

"Non-Whaling" Boat Activity

In addition to searching for whales, several Nuiqsut whaling vessels made trips between Cross Island and West Dock. Generally, after the harvest of a whale a certain portion of it is sent to Nuiqsut to "feed the village." In most cases the successful captain will designate one or more of his crew members to take one of his boats to Nuiqsut for this purpose. In 2003, for the first whale, the "fresh kill" was actually sent to West Dock via an Alaska Clean Seas ferry that happened to be making a trip to Cross Island the day after the whale was harvested. The captain arranged for it to be flown to Nuiqsut from there. The captain's youngest son accompanied the muktuk and meat so that he could "run the flag" from the airport to the captain's house. For the next two whales, both taken on 9/05, boats made trips to Nuiqsut the next day (9/06) specifically for this purpose. Both returned the day after that (9/07), but one immediately made a return trip to Nuiqsut with another load, since its crew had taken another whale in the meantime. This boat returned two days later (9/09) so that it could help the crew leave at the end of the season on 9/10.

This information collection effort focuses explicitly on Cross Island whaling activity. No attempt was made to collect information on preparation, support, or other crew member activities that occurred elsewhere (primarily in Nuiqsut). Similarly, although whaling support activities from non-Nuiqsut sources (mainly oil and gas industry support through Alaska Clean Seas barges) were quite evident, both in terms of island infrastructure as well as the frequency of ACS barge activity, they were not logged in detail. During the 19-day period when whalers were on Cross Island, one or more ACS barges landed on Cross Island at least four times, primarily to provide logistical support to the whalers. In addition, at least one (and probably several) ACS barges landed on Cross Island prior to 8/23 in order to mobilize the generator, bring over the loader, and other support materials. ACS barges of course were used to demobilize these items, which took place the day the last crew left Cross Island on 9/10/03. Conditions were poor for small-boat travel, so that the boats for this crew were also loaded on the large barge for transport to West Dock, and crew members were transported in smaller ASC ferries. The crew stayed overnight at the Prudhoe Bay Hotel and most of them continued on to Nuiqsut by boat the next day. One Boat broke a steering cable and was trucked to Oliktok Point (for eventual pickup) while its boat crew of two flew from Deadhorse to Nuiqsut. Documentation of contacts and interactions through telephone, FAX, or non-whaling non-Nuiqsut vessel were not fully documented, and such information was only collected as contextual background.

GPS Information

In terms of GPS locational information, all whaling crews agreed to carry and use GPS units. The level of information obtained varied from boat to boat, as discussed above, but for most boats and for all crews at least partial tracking information (where most boats went each day) was obtained, along with the unlabeled points where whales were observed (or struck). In Table 4, as discussed above, the days that boats went out whaling are shaded. Dark shading indicates that a GPS track was not obtained for that day from that boat. Light shading indicates that a GPS track was obtained form that boat for that day. It should be noted that there were 34 potential different "boat days" for which GPS tracks could have been collected (a marked decrease in effort from both 2001 and 2002). GPS tracks were collected for 30 boat days, or 88 percent of all 34 potential boat days (96 percent of all boat days once the researcher was on Cross Island). Of the 4 "boat days" (12 percent of all potential boat days) for which GPS tracks were not collected, 3 were for days before the observer was on Cross Island. All GPS tracks collected have been transmitted to MMS in Garmin MapSource (*.MPS) format and can be viewed using MapSource or other standard GIS and mapping software. A composite map showing all tracks collected is included below (Figure 6).

A list of all waypoints noted by Nuiqsut whaling crews is presented in Table 5. Not all were actually marked by crews while they were out on the water. Some were described by crews during their reviews of GPS tracks. Thus, not all whale sightings were marked, and not all unmarked whale sightings were later described to the researcher. The daily boat report forms do include some additional likely whale sightings that are not included in Table 6, but these additional points are based on whalers' general accounts, and no specific locational information. It is likely that not all whale sightings are included on the daily report forms, although most individual whales sighted are probably represented. Multiple sightings of the same whale were usually reported as such by most crews, but most crews only marked a single position for a whale unless they followed it for a significant period of time and/or struck it. Different crews marked the position of the same whale, so the number of different whales observed would be difficult to determine without an analysis of all points and tracks in relation to each other.

Waypoints are of three types – whale sightings/strikes, reference points (generally whales seen on previous days or by other boats), and "unknown significance". Whale sightings may have actually been marked by a crew, or may have been located on their track when reviewing it with the researcher at some point. Strike locations are relatively fixed, but sightings may be for a whale or blow located anywhere from 10 feet to several miles from the boat, and thus are less fixed in terms of position. Each waypoint number consists of three parts: BoatID (upper case for points marked while out on the water, lower case for points located while discussing the GPS track with the researcher), Date(mmddyy), and Sequence Number.

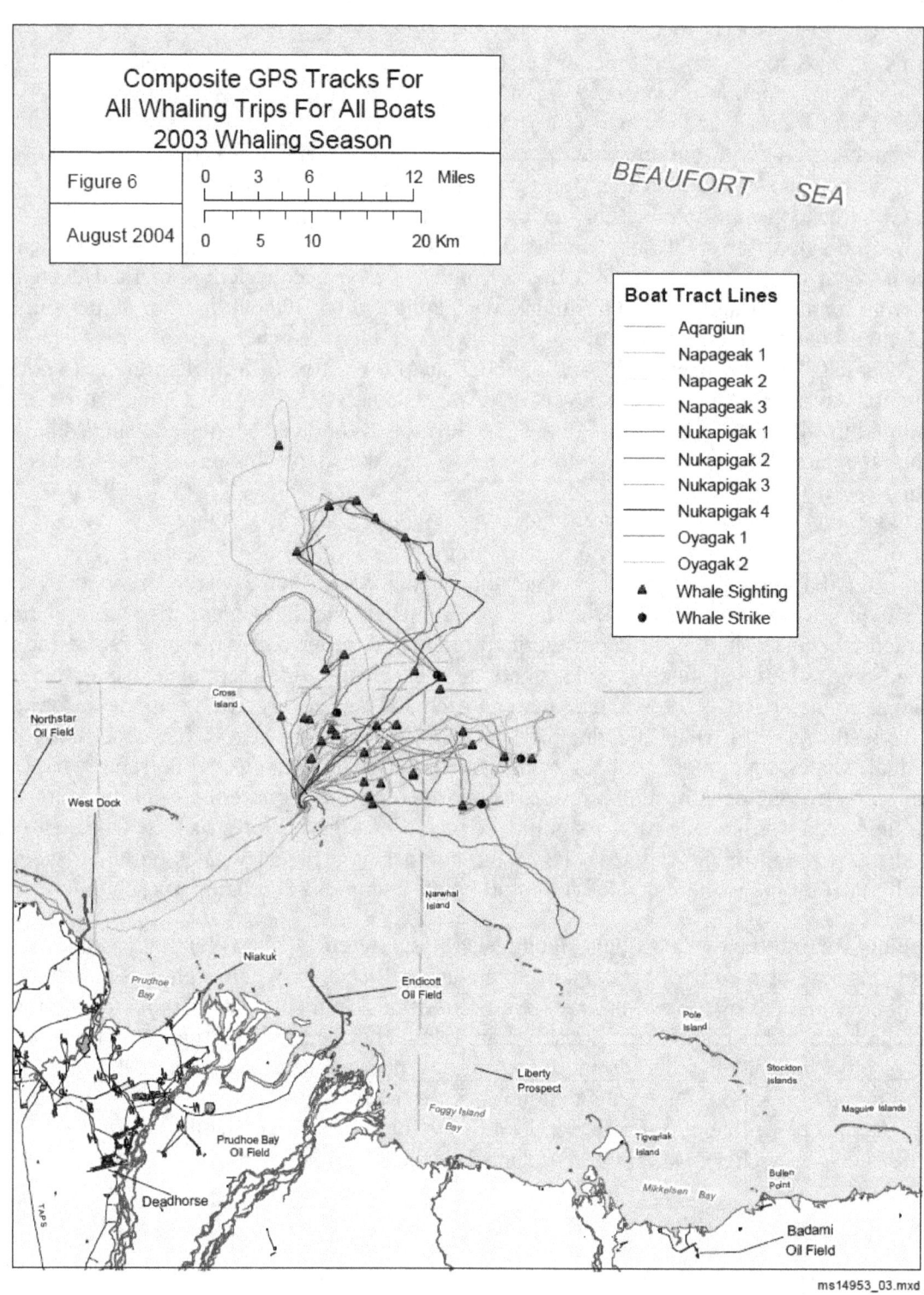

Composite GPS Tracks For
All Whaling Trips For All Boats
2003 Whaling Season

Figure 6	0 3 6 12 Miles
August 2004	0 5 10 20 Km

Boat Tract Lines

Aqargiun
Napageak 1
Napageak 2
Napageak 3
Nukapigak 1
Nukapigak 2
Nukapigak 3
Nukapigak 4
Oyagak 1
Oyagak 2
▲ Whale Sighting
● Whale Strike

BEAUFORT   SEA

ms14953_03.mxd

Table 5: Waypoints of 2003

Date	Crew	Lat/Long	Way Point #	Time	Notes
08/25/03	Napageak	N70 46.670 W148 03.764	nap3_082503a	NA	Reported whale sighting – no time available
08/25/03	Napageak	N70 36.999 W147 50.599	nap3_082503b	6:00 PM	Resumed high speed (20-30 mph) to return to Cross Island
08/27/03	Napageak	N70 31.849 W147 58.916	nap1_082703a	3:52 PM	3 miles from CI, a jog to the east (no real change in speed)
08/27/03	Napageak	N70 33.106 W148 00.861	nap1_082703b	4:15 PM	4.5 miles from CI, slow to 4-8 mph
08/27/03	Napageak	N70 33.578 W147 59.158	nap1_082703c	5:19 PM	5.0 miles from CI, slow to 3- mph, soon resumed 4-8 mph
08/27/03	Napageak	N70 32.444 W148 00.188	nap1_082703d	5:36 PM	3.7 miles from CI, resume faster speed, probably heading back to Cross Island
08/27/03	Napageak	N70 33.190 W148 05.511	nap3_082703a	1:44 PM	Up to this point, NAP3 had been at slow scouting speed (below 5 mph). From this point until return to Cross Island, NAP3 was at fast scouting speed (5-10 mph).
08/27/03	Napageak	N70 32.463 W148 00.179	nap3_082703b	5:36 PM	Most of this trip spent at 5-10 mph (with brief spurts of higher speed), but from this point at higher speeds – probably returning to Cross Island
09/01/03	Aqargiun	N70 32.434 W147 53.383	IAN_090103a	12:27 PM	Coordinates given to another boat so that they could meet
09/01/03	Aqargiun	N70 33.047 W147 55.077	IAN_090103b	12:36 PM	Report that this is where they struck the whale, but the time and other aspects are inconsistent. Probably where they first saw the whale.
09/01/03	Aqargiun	N70 33.853 W147 54.351	ian_090103c	12:55 PM	Likely coordinates for whale strike
09/01/03	Aqargiun	N70 33.530 W147 56.129	IAN_090103d	1:48 PM	Coordinates for where whale was killed
09/01/03	Napageak	N70 29.844 W147 49.367	NAP1_090103a	11:17 AM	Unknown significance
09/01/03	Napageak	N70 33.276 W147 48.380	nap1_090103b	11:59 AM	Area where speed reduced, met NAP2
09/01/03	Napageak	N70 32.473 W147 56.616	nap1_090103c	12:19 PM	Position where speed reduced (until next waypoint)
09/01/03	Napageak	N70 31.614 W147 58.029	nap1_090103d	12:38 PM	Position where speed increased (until next waypoint)
09/01/03	Napageak	N70 32.415 W147 59.486	nap1_090103e	12:43 PM	Position where speed reduced (until next waypoint)
09/01/03	Napageak	N70 32.988 W147 58.901	nap1_090103f	12:52 PM	Position where speed increased (until next waypoint) – probably responding to IAN strike
09/01/03	Napageak	N70 33.734 W147 55.043	nap1_090103g	12:57 PM	Speed decreased, near IAN whale strike waypoint
09/01/03	Napageak	N70 30.480 W147 47.676	NAP2_090103a	11:31 AM	Significance unclear. May be a reference point used on 9/05/03
09/01/03	Napageak	N70 30.472 W147 47.658	NAP2_090103b	11:31 AM	Significance unclear. May be a reference point used on 9/05/03
09/01/03	Oyagak	N70 33.924 W147 54.257	bo1_090103a	12:55 PM	Position at time of float attachment (in support)
09/01/03	Oyagak	N70 33.522 W147 56.184	bo1_090103b	1:48 PM	Position at time of kill (in support)
09/01/03	Oyagak	N70 33.847 W147 54.382	bo2_090103a	12:55 PM	Position at time of float attachment (in support)
09/01/03	Oyagak	N70 33.598 W147 55.488	BO2_090103b	1:20 PM	Marked during whale chase
09/01/03	Oyagak	N70 33.527 W147 56.134	bo2_090103c	1:48 PM	Position at time of kill (in support)

Table 5: Waypoints of 2003 (Continued)

Date	Crew	Lat/Long	Way Point #	Time	Notes
09/02/03	Napageak	N70 29.455 W147 59.035	NAP3_090203a	NA	Evidently marked on Cross Island for some reason
09/02/03	Napageak	N70 31.504 W147 46.894	NAP3_090203b	NA	Reference point? – not on track
09/02/03	Napageak	N70 30.996 W147 42.834	nap3_090203c	7:14PM	Whale sighting (reported, not marked by crew)
09/02/03	Napageak	N70 31.854 W147 35.757	nap3_090203d	7:35PM	NAP3 position when called by another boat that had seen a whale (NAP3 never saw this whale)
09/02/03	Napageak	N70 33.763 W147 29.497	nap3_090203e	8:53PM	Position when they decided to return to Cross Island
09/02/03	Nukapigak	N70 32.795 W147 54.517	nuk1_090203a	5:54PM	Radio report that they saw a whale – but later radio back that it was a log. This prompts the other boats to go out anyway.
09/02/03	Nukapigak	N70 32.397 W147 33.993	NUK1_090203b	8:00PM	Whale sighting – no other details
09/02/03	Oyagak	N70 33.042 W147 35.464	bo2_090203a	7:45 PM	Saw whale, 30-33', chased it. 2 smaller whales in front of it, maybe 1 mile
09/02/03	Oyagak	N70 31.854 W147 29.301	BO2_090203b	8:09 PM	Missed strike on above whale
09/03/03	Nukapigak	N70 33.638 W148 02.696	nuk2_090303a	5:52 AM	About 5 miles out, possible blow – many whalebirds
09/03/03	Nukapigak	N70 35.935 W147 56.170	nuk2_090303b	7:24 AM	Point where NAP3 radioed them that they saw a whale
09/03/03	Nukapigak	N70 36.640 W147 53.428	NUK3_090303a	7:32AM	Whale sighting – no other details
09/05/03	Aqargiun	N70 32.295 W147 46.782	ian_090503a	6:26 AM	Position when IAN slowed to look for whales because NAP2 had seen one. NAP2 was to the south of IAN boat somewhat more than 1 mile.
09/05/03	Aqargiun	N70 31.661 W147 35.033	ian_090503b	6:26 AM	Position where IAN resumed "traveling" speed – possibly because they were called to a whale NAP2 was following.
09/05/03	Aqargiun	N70 29.486 W147 35.360	IAN_090503c	7:07 AM	Reported as position IAN struck the whale. It is more consistent with radio reports and other accounts that this is a sighting waypoint.
09/05/03	Aqargiun	N70 29.574 W147 32.571	IAN_090503d	7:13 AM	Reported as where IAN bat had to turn around 180 degrees. More consistent that this is where the whale was first struck.
09/05/03	Aqargiun	N70 29.663 W147 32.467	ian_090503e	7:32 AM	Likely IAN position when NAP2 put in 2nd darting gun bomb
09/05/03	Aqargiun	N70 29.666 W147 32.423	ian_090503f	7:38 AM	Likely IAN position when IAN killed whale with shoulder gun bomb
09/05/03	Aqargiun	N70 29.622 W147 32.295	IAN_090503g	7:52 AM	Reported as position IAN had to turn around again. More consistent as location of radio report of killed whale
09/05/03	Aqargiun	N70 29.468 W147 31.571	ian_090503h	8:02 AM	IAN position at time of reported start of tow
09/05/03	Napageak	N70 34.048 W147 23.003	NAP1_090503a	10:08 AM	Position marked for NAP3 whale (kill)
09/05/03	Napageak	N70 33.799 W147 21.878	nap1_090503b	11:18 AM	Position of start of tow (approximate)
09/05/03	Napageak	N70 30.628 W147 47.419	nap2_090503a	6:26 AM	NAP2 position at time IAN crew reported spotting a whale (no direct confirmation of this from the NAP2 crew). Possible sighting of whale, could be the same as whale for waypoint "d"
09/05/03	Napageak	N70 30.900 W147 42.788	NAP2_090503b	6:37 AM	Labeled "Whale" so almost certainly a whale sighting, probable following

Table 5: Waypoints of 2003 (Continued)

Date	Crew	Lat/Long	Way Point #	Time	Notes
09/05/03	Napageak	N70 29.310 W147 34.077	NAP2_090503c	7:12 AM	NAP2 position at some time as IAN at IAN_090503c (sighting or strike of whale – see IAN report). Turned around and helped to follow IAN whale – may have been trying to spot it at first before NAP2 and IAN boats came together. This point was marked by the crew, but with no clear explanation.
09/05/03	Napageak	N70 29.628 W147 32.373	nap2_090503d	7:38 AM	Probable position when NAP2 struck whale with 2nd darting gun bomb
09/05/03	Napageak	N70 34.058 W147 23.375	NAP2_090503e	10:04 AM	Essentially the same point, marking NAP3 whale (near kill location)
09/05/03	Napageak	N70 34.057 W147 23.315	NAP2_090503f	10:07 AM	Essentially the same point, marking NAP3 whale (near kill location)
09/05/03	Napageak	N70 30.551 W147 50.159	NAP3_090503a	NA	Marked by crew, significance not known
09/05/03	Napageak	N70 31.767 W147 26.849	nap3_090503b	8:06 AM	Likely location of initial NAP3 strike (harpoon & float/no bomb)
09/05/03	Nukapigak	N70 29.467 W147 48.855	nuk2_090503a	6:06 AM	Point where two "currents" (contours) meet – see notes
09/05/03	Nukapigak	N70 29.487 W147 35.360	NUK2_090503b	8:56 AM	Point marked as reference point of IAN whale (dead). Probably marked about 7:20 AM while NUK2 and NUK3 still some distance away.
09/05/03	Oyagak	N70 34.025 W147 23.538	bo1_090503a	9:55 AM	Position when BO advised them to go for a "hard" shot (a chest shot) on the NAP whale, as it was still strong even with several bombs already delivered to the normal kill area
09/05/03	Oyagak	N70 31.968 W147 50.294	bo2_090503a	6:23 AM	Position where BO2 slowed markedly, usually indicating sighting a whale or increased search effort
09/05/03	Oyagak	N70 33.146 W147 37.399	bo2_090503b	7:07 AM	Position where BO2 increased speed and changed direction to join IAN crew, clearly in response to someone [NAP2?] spotting a whale
09/05/03	Oyagak	N70 29.469 W147 35.268	bo2_090503c	7:14 AM	Position where BO2 slows again, to join in chase of ON whale – very close to position as where IAN marked whale (reported to be strike – more likely marks a sighting)
09/05/03	Oyagak	N70 29.548 W147 31.916	bo2_090503d	7:24 AM	Area of probable strike area for IAN whale – BO2 in the area 7:25-7:33 AM, then leaves to scout for more whales
09/05/03	Oyagak	N70 32.248 W147 29.776	bo2_090503e	8:02 AM	Area where NAP3 whale may have been 1st seen - by BO2?
09/05/03	Oyagak	N70 31.854 W147 29.301	BO2_090503f	NA	Reference point for this whale?
09/05/03	Oyagak	N70 31.767 W147 26.849	bo2_090503g	8:06 AM	Likely location of initial NAP3 strike (harpoon/no bomb)
09/05/03	Oyagak	N70 31.771 W147 25.184	BO2_090503h	8:24 AM	Chasing NAP3 whale – many bombs put into this whale. May be the area of the initial strike (harpoon/no bomb)
09/05/03	Oyagak	N70 34.001 W147 23.612	bo2_090503i	9:55 AM	Chasing NAP3 whale, near the end – one of the last shots

Table 5: Waypoints of 2003 (Continued)

Date	Crew	Lat/Long	Way Point #	Time	Notes
09/06/03	Napageak	N70 33.316 W147 45.405	NAP2_090603a	7:45 PM	Unknown significance – reported to simply have dropped the GPS (and unit was then off for about a minute)
09/06/03	Napageak	N70 35.900 W147 42.788	nap2_090603b	7:55 PM	Reported that this was the approximate location when they first saw the whale – they did not mark the point, however
09/06/03	Napageak	N70 35.729 W147 39.428	nap2_090603c	8:18 PM	Time reported for strike – position taken from GPS track
09/06/03	Napageak	N70 35.661 W147 39.160	nap2_090603d	8:36 PM	Time of radio announcement of successful kill – position taken from GPS track
09/06/03	Nukapigak	N70 41.555 W148 00.748	NUK3_090603a	8:17 PM	Whale they were following (also marked by other boats)
09/06/03	Nukapigak	N70 42.329 W147 44.478	NUK4_090603a	7:09 PM	Reported as 2nd sighting of this first whale
09/06/03	Nukapigak	N70 44.074 W147 52.006	NUK4_090603b	7:27 PM	Report sighting many whales – 10 or more, as close as .25 miles to boat, and as far as 4 miles to the NW
09/06/03	Nukapigak	N70 35.044 W147 39.039	NUK4_090603c	8:33 PM	Reported as the first sighting of the first whale of the day. Given distance from point "a" this seems unlikely—some error would seem to be involved.
09/06/03	Nukapigak	N70 35.645 W147 38.716	NUK4_090603d	9:11 PM	NUP2 whale
09/06/03	Oyagak	N70 44.101 W147 52.040	bo1_090603a	7:26 PM	Area where whale(s) seen and looked for
09/06/03	Oyagak	N70 43.749 W147 56.963	bo1_090603b	8:36 PM	Following at least 2 whales – radio report/communication
09/06/03	Oyagak	N70 41.394 W148 00.307	bo1_090603c	8:12 PM	Radio report of bigger blows than before (may be different)
09/06/03	Oyagak	N70 41.283 W148 00.717	bo1_090603d	8:17 PM	Position when NAP2 struck whale, they went to assist
09/06/03	Oyagak	N70 36.426 W147 41.897	bo1_090603e	8:38 PM	Position when radio announcement of killed whale
09/06/03	Oyagak	N70 35.621 W147 38.765	bo1_090603f	9:31 PM	Approximate start of tow
09/06/03	Oyagak	N70 33.485 W147 58.403	bo2_090603a	5:55 PM	BO2 position when they slowed and turned NE to scout for whale spotted by BO1 and NUK2
09/06/03	Oyagak	N70 36.076 W147 49.067	bo2_090603b	6:34 PM	BO2 position when they gave up on this whale
09/06/03	Oyagak	N70 40.511 W147 42.018	BO2_090603c	6:59 PM	Whale spotted – may have been same as NUK2 followed
09/06/03	Oyagak	N70 43.236 W147 48.959	BO2_090603d	7:15 PM	Different whale, somewhat smaller – lose it quickly
09/06/03	Oyagak	N70 43.795 W147 56.071	BO2_090603e	7:35 PM	Two more different whales, 1 medium-sized and 1 smaller. Saw about 5 other blows in this area as well.
09/06/03	Oyagak	N70 41.272 W148 00.163	bo2_090603f	8:17 PM	BO2 position (chasing whale) when called to assist NAP2
09/06/03	Oyagak	N70 35.634 W147 38.758	BO2_090603g	9:25 PM	NAP2 whale (harvest location) – arrived to assist with the chase about 8:40 PM

NOTES: CAPITAL letters in the Waypoint # indicate a waypoint marked by a crew while they were scouting for whales.
Lower case letters in a Waypoint # indicate a waypoint of interest pointed out by a crew while reviewing their GPS track with the researcher
Lack of a time for a waypoint indicates that the point was not marked or that the track for that day was flawed

Other Subsistence Activities

Very little non-whaling subsistence activity was documented on or near Cross Island during the whaling season, although of course a great deal of "non-whaling" subsistence activity took place throughout the year in order to support the whaling effort. Whalers did note that they had seen seals and birds, but did not mark these points and generally described such sightings as taking place where ice was encountered (which was not often). Polar bears were first seen on Cross Island 09/01/03 (the day the first whale was taken) and it can be presumed were present from that point on. Several bears approached those butchering the whale and had to be scared away with gunshots. Four bears were seen 9/01, and at least six the next day. A few boat trips were taken to look around for seal or ducks, but no harvest occurred.

Nuiqsut Whalers' Observations and Perceptions of Whale Behavior in 2003

Ice conditions in 2003 were more moderate than in 2001 or 2002, but the weather prevented scouting more than 50 percent of the time whalers were on Cross Island. High wind (and the lack of ice that could have moderated the effect of the wind) was the major weather factor cited by the whalers. Whalers reported encountering small patches of ice only sporadically. Weather prevented scouting for whales on seven days (and parts of others), as opposed to nine in 2001 and four in 2002. Thus, while conditions were not as optimal as they had been in 2000, or even as good as in 2002, they may have been better or about the same as for 2001. Level of effort, as measured by time spent out on the water, was much less in 2003 than in 2002 or 2001. In terms of the same factors about which Nuiqsut whalers made observations in 2001 and 2002:

- Nuiqsut whalers reported seeing more whales during hunting trips in 2003 than in 2002, and quite a few more than in 2001. Whales were observed on every day that boats went out scouting.
- Nuiqsut whalers could find whales relatively close to Cross Island (6 to 8 miles) but could not always follow these whales. Whales could consistently be found within 10 to 20 miles. Whales were harvested closer to Cross Island in 2003 than in 2001 or 2002. Whalers took shorter trips, both in terms of length and time duration, than in 2002 or 2001
- No whaler explicitly mentioned observing skittish or "spooky" whale behavior .

All whales struck were killed and recovered – none sunk or were otherwise problematic.

Planned Future Activities

As this is written, the final report for the original Task 4 of the ANIMIDA program, discussing the 2001 and 2002 field seasons, has been submitted to the sponsor and copies distributed to local participants in Nuiqsut (and the AEWC in Barrow). The only remaining tasks for the ANIMIDA project thus consist of this annual report for 2003, and all tasks will be complete once this draft is reviewed, revised, and accepted as final. Three more field seasons (2004-2006) for this project have been funded as part of the cANIMIDA project. Data collection for the 2004 field season has been successfully completed. For the immediate future, the following tasks will be of most importance:

- Finalization of the 2003 Annual Report.

- Data processing and reporting of 2004 data. All GPS tracks have been processed. Daily boat report forms remain to be finalized, and their format will probably be changed so that the activities of all boats are recorded together for the same day. This will have two beneficial effects. It will simplify the recording process and reduce the number of forms to be completed, since days of no whaling activity will not require any forms. It will also make the interaction among boats, and the relationships between the waypoints noted by the different crews, more obvious than the earlier system of separate forms for each boat. Primary analysis of crew composition and basic descriptive statistics of whaling activity has been completed.

- Field assistant recruitment and training. A trip to Nuiqsut (and probably Barrow) will be scheduled for summer of 2005, and will have this task as one of its goals. This aspect of the project has been problematic to this point.

- This trip will also be used to present the results of the 2003 (and probably 2004) field seasons to the Nuiqsut Whaling Captains Association, and to the community at large if desired, and to ask for permission to conduct research at Cross Island in 2005. Attempts to make preliminary arrangements for the 2005 research will also begin at this time.

- Draft annual report for 2004. Work on this report has begun. It is unlikely that a draft will be ready before the summer trip to Nuiqsut, although material be available for a presentation to the NWCA. Graphics for this report (and subsequent reports) will be prepared in-house to facilitate their design and modification. In-house GIS capability will also enhance the eventual analytical report after the 2006 (or 2007) field season.

- 2005 data collection on Cross Island.

References Cited

Brown, William E.
1979   Nuiqsut Paisanich: Nuiqsut Heritage, a Cultural Plan. Prepared for the Village of Nuiqsut and the North Slope Borough Planning Commission and Commission on History and Culture: Barrow.

Carnahan, John
1979   Cross Island: Inupiat Cultural Continuum. North Slope Borough: Anchorage.

Dumond, Don E.
1984   Prehistory of the Bering Sea region. *In* Handbook of North American Indians, Volume 5: Arctic (pages 94-105). David Damas, editor. Smithsonian Institution: Washington D.C.

Galginaitis, Michael
1990   Subsistence Resource Harvest Patterns: Nuiqsut. Special Report No. 8. OCS Study MMS 90-0038. Prepared by Impact Assessment Inc. for the United States Department of the Interior, Minerals Management Service, Alaska OCS Region: Anchorage.

Galginaitis, Michael; Claudia Chang; Kathleen M. MacQueen; Albert A. Dekin; and David Zipkin
1984   Ethnographic Study and Monitoring Methodology of Contemporary Economic Growth, Socio-Cultural Change and Community Development in Nuiqsut, Alaska. Technical Report No. 96. Minerals Management Service, Alaska Outer Continental Shelf Region, Leasing and Environment Office, Social and Economic Studies Unit. Anchorage.

Galginaitis, Michael and Dale Funk.
2003b   Annual Assessment of Subsistence Bowhead Whaling Near Cross Island: 2002 – ANIMIDA Task Order 4. Prepared for the Minerals management Service, Alaska OCS Region, United States Department of the Interior. Revised April 2004.

Galginaitis, Michael and Dale Funk.
2004   Annual Assessment of Subsistence Bowhead Whaling Near Cross Island: 2001 and 2002 – ANIMIDA Task Order 4 Final Report. Prepared for the Minerals management Service, Alaska OCS Region, United States Department of the Interior.

Galginaitis, Michael and Dale Funk.
2005   Draft Annual Assessment of Subsistence Bowhead Whaling Near Cross Island: 2003 – ANIMIDA Task Order 4. Prepared for the Minerals management Service, Alaska OCS Region, United States Department of the Interior. In the process of finalization.

Hoffman, David; David Libbey; and Grant Spearman
1986   Nuiqsut: Land Use Values Through Time in the Nuiqsut Area. North Slope
       Borough: Barrow. Originally published in 1978 as Occasional Paper No. 12 by
       Anthropology and Historic Preservation Cooperative Park Studies Unit,
       University of Alaska: Fairbanks.

Huntington, Henry P.
1992   Wildlife Management and Subsistence Hunting in Alaska. University of
       Washington Press: Seattle.

Krupnik, Igor and Sam Stoker
1993   Subsistence Whaling. In J.J.Burns and J.J.Montague (eds.). The Bowhead Whale.
       Society for Marine Biology, Special Publication 2, p.579-630.

Long, Frank Jr.
1996   History of Subsistence Whaling by Nuiqsut in Proceedings of the 1995 Arctic
       Synthesis Meeting. OCS Study MMS 95-0065, pages 73-76. United States
       Department of the Interior, Minerals Management Service, Alaska OCS Region:
       Anchorage.

McCartney, Allen P.
1994   Whale size selection by precontact hunters of the North American western arctic
       and subarctic. In Hunting the Largest Animals: Native Whaling in the Western
       Arctic and Subarctic, edited by A.P. McCartney, pp. 83-108, Studies in Whaling
       No. 3, Occasional Paper No. 36, Circumpolar Institute, University of Alberta,
       Edmonton.

Rexford, Burton
1997   A Native's View. Presented at a workshop sponsored by the Department of the
       Interior, Minerals Management Service, Alaska OCS Region, in Barrow, Alaska.
       http://www.mms.gov/alaska/native/rexford/rexford.htm

Smith, Roy J. (editor)
1980   Qiniqtuagaksrat Utuqqanaat Inuuniagninisiqun: The Traditional Land Use
       Inventory for the Mid-Beaufort Sea, Volume 1. North Slope Borough
       Commission on History and Culture: Barrow.

United States Department of Commerce, National Oceanic and Atmospheric
Administration, National Marine Fisheries Service
1977   International Whaling Commission's Deletion of Native Exemption for the
       Subsistence Harvest of Bowhead Whales: Final Environmental Impact Statement.
       Two Volumes. United States Department of Commerce, National Oceanic and
       Atmospheric Administration, np.
1978   Bowhead Whales: A Special Report to the International Whaling Commission.
       United States Department of Commerce, National Oceanic and Atmospheric
       Administration: np.

Wohlforth, Charles P.
2004   The Whale and the Supercomputer: On the Northern Front of Climate Change.
        North Point Press, PLACE.

Worl, Rosita
1979   The North Slope Inupiat whaling complex *in* Alaska Native Culture and History.
        Yoshinobu Kotani and William B. Workman, editors. Papers presented at the
        International Symposium on the Culture History of the Alaska Natives (1978).
        Senri Ethnological Studies, Volume 4. National Museum of Ethnology: Osaka.

Electronic Appendices

Annual Assessment of Subsistence Bowhead Whaling Near Cross Island, 2003 Annual
Report (ANIMIDA Task 4) – PDF file "AnRpt2003.pdf"

Data Logger file from Cross Island weather station for 2003 in Excel format – file
"CI2003WF,xls"

PDF format files containing displays of individual and combined whale boat GPS tracks
for all days on which at least one boat went scouting for whales:
"AppendixA.pdf"

PDF format file containing all boat report forms for 2003:
"AppendixB.pdf"